Writ

WA

Writing
Popular
Fiction

Books in the 'Writing Handbooks' series

Other books for writers

Writing Handbooks

Writing Popular Fiction

SECOND EDITION

Rona Randall

A & C Black • London

Second edition 1997
First published 1992

A & C Black (Publishers) Limited
35 Bedford Row, London WC1R 4JH

0–7136–4731-0

A CIP catalogue record for this book is available from
the British Library.

Typeset in 10½ on 12½ pt Sabon
Printed and bound in Great Britain by
Creative Print and Design (Wales), Ebbw Vale

Contents

Acknowledgements

To that renowned Editor, the late Harold Snoad,
and to his Literary Editor, the legendary Dorothy Sutherland,
whose combined faith in me – and encouragement –
led to my long career as an author.

1. The Way to Authorship

Signposts and warnings

This book is written for people who want to become authors but don't know how to get started; for those who are already trying but are despairing; for those who have become discouraged by rejection; for those who have enrolled for tuition classes and drifted away either uninspired or deflated and believing that the fault lies in themselves, that they were never 'meant' to be authors; for those who, conversely, think they have only to attend creative writing courses for immediate publication to be guaranteed; and for those who have experienced a small measure of success, wish to advance further, but have somehow become stuck.

It is also written for those who imagine the job to be easy and a surefire way of making big money quickly. They have a lot to learn.

After spending virtually the whole of my adult life in non-stop professional authorship in a world of ever-changing public tastes, I believe aspiring authors can be helped to master the craft, but that it cannot be taught as some occupations are taught. Any branch of writing, and particularly fiction, is not a scientific or mathematical process which, once learned, will earn a string of letters after your name. Writing is a skill you will continue to learn for the whole of your life, but guidelines can act as signposts to set you on the right course and keep you there.

The guidelines I offer throughout this book should make the going less rough and steer you to success, providing you really want to achieve it.

I offer no magic formula, because there is none. In the final analysis it is you, the aspiring author, who wields the magic wand. Yours is the imagination, the love of words, the urge to create, the desire, the diligence, the dedication – and the self-discipline. These are the tools you need; you must use them and never neglect them. My aim is to show you *how* to use them, and to convince you that you *can* do it even when hope is at a low ebb.

There is one other vital tool which every aspiring author needs. Enthusiasm. Without it, no author's work will ever reach the popularity lists because enthusiasm is infectious; the reader catches it and awaits your next book eagerly. Thus a readership is built up and maintained. Lose that enthusiasm and you will lose your readers and, in consequence, your publishers.

But that is not going to happen to you, because if you lacked enthusiasm you would not be reading this book.

Coupled with that essential quality is another to which few aspiring authors ever give a thought – self-honesty. By that I mean acknowledging the truth about your personal motivation. Ask yourself *why* you want to write. If your only answer is 'Money!' then you are not a compulsive writer. Even if you do sell some of your work you are unlikely to stay the course, because when you discover that authorship is as unpredictable as any other form of self-employment, you will quit and seek a more stable job.

'But', you argue, 'look at the gigantic sums paid to best-selling authors!'

Unfortunately, that is as far as the general public does look, because that is the only side to attract attention from the press. The bulk of hard-working, full-time authors, who form the major part of the profession, never achieve such publicity, but they would not abandon the work for any other because writing is the breath of life to them and, despite its demands on time and the sacrifice of much social life (five-day weeks are virtually unknown to full-time writers), they want no other career because this one brings the greatest sense of fulfilment – which is what every real author writes for. Call it ego-gratification if you wish. He, or she, *must* write, or mentally stifle.

This applies to every branch of creativity. You have only to delve into the lives of past authors or artists or musicians to discover endless examples. What compelled Van Gogh or Gauguin to paint despite their sufferings, or Beethoven to compose when he could not hear a note of his music, or the Brontë sisters to write even when publication seemed an impossible dream? This passionate need for self-expression is in every writer who yearns to make authorship his or her career, no matter at what level – intellectual or non-intellectual.

This is not to say that money doesn't act as an impetus to output, but its value to writers is the freedom it brings to work in their own way, in their own time, at the job they most want to do. It is exciting to hit the jackpot, but for many authors who achieve a steady, well-paid and very satisfactory living, jackpots are unknown. In my own experience, I was a steady-selling hardback author with a big British publishing house for years before rocketing bids in New York for two of my titles – *Dragonmede* and *The Watchman's Stone* – sent their sales soaring world-wide. Since then greater sums have been paid, some well deserved but many disastrously, for material no self-respecting author would submit and from which their publishers learned severe lessons. When such things happen, the real professionals keep their feet on the ground and continue, purposefully, to write.

I have sometimes wondered whether I would have been spared a great deal of stress if I had not had such an experience, even though my ranking as an author went up and so did publishers' terms thereafter, but the pressure to repeat the mixture-as-before was not for me. This raises the question of whether it is wiser to stay with one particular genre, or to diversify, writing various types of fiction under varying names (as many writers do). Once you are launched, the choice must be yours.

In my own case it so happened that, with the characteristic unpredictability of the publishing world, fashions in fiction suddenly changed and the popularity of the gothic, the genre in which I won this success, eventually faded so I was glad I had followed my instinct and continued to write what I wanted to write. I stayed in the marketplace, under my own name, with period novels like *The Mating Dance, The Ladies of Hanover Square,* and *The Drayton Legacy.* When and if you find yourself in a like situation, you must must decide whether to go with the stream or continue to write only what you want to write and what you know you do best.

Fashions in fiction

It may be surprising to learn that fashions in reading matter can change. There can be various reasons for this. New television soap operas, setting new trends, can be one. Strong commercial hype by a publisher for a new type of story by a new name can be another. Or, as with the gothic – a genre launched by Horace

Walpole's *Castle of Otranto* in 1746 and revived by Charlotte Brontë's *Jane Eyre* in 1847 – the market can become flooded with badly written, badly constructed and badly plotted imitations produced by speculative publishers aiming to jump on the band-wagon. In such a case the public's interest becomes satiated, sales fall, and the market disappears.

Currently, this has happened to historical novels, despite the resurgence on television of classics like *Pride and Prejudice*. Written before copyright existed, its first publisher was able to buy the novel outright for £100 and people have grown rich on it ever since. This may account for the upsurge of stage and screen dramatisations of pre-copyright works, but not for the down-trend in sales of historical fiction. The fact that a number of well established publishers have ceased publishing it, and agents to handle it, speaks for itself – as does the increased borrowing of library videos and the decreased borrowing of fiction, confirming that people are reading less and screen-watching more. This may be fine for television dramatists, but not for others.

Mercifully, tides can turn as swiftly as fashions and a down-trend in one genre always seems to be counterbalanced by an up-trend in another. Only the contemporary novel seems never to lose favour, so if you are in harmony with the present day and can write about it with authenticity and enjoyment, you have little to fear.

Meanwhile, there is a market for the historically-dedicated. Paperback publishers Harlequin Mills & Boon have a category (amongst their plentiful lists) for short historical romances, so if you are anxious to hone your craft while waiting for the tide to turn, you could do worse than study the guidelines of such well established paperback publishers.

But your aims are higher? Good. Always aim high, but don't regret it if you have to take it a step at a time, and don't be apologetic if your aim is merely to entertain. In a world filled with increasing stress and pain and cruelty, what better occup-ation can there be than one which brings enjoyment to thousands of people? One of my greatest rewards came a few years ago, mailed to me care of my publishers – an envelope with a Glasgow postmark containing a scrap of paper on which was written, very simply, 'Thank you for all the enjoyment your books have given me.' It bore no address and no signature, and accompanying it was a Scottish pound note. I have never parted with either. That kindly gesture has been kept as a talisman ever since. My only regret is that I have never been able to thank that unknown reader.

If, along the way, you experience a moment like that, you will know the joy of being an author.

Taking the first steps

There is a school of thought which insists that writers are born, not made; that no one can become a successful author by studying textbooks or attending creative writing classes; that every writer must be his or her own tutor, learning as they go (which means learning as they write and write). The parentheses are mine because I know that constant writing does indeed mean constant learning, but the rest I consider to be unduly sceptical.

Not surprisingly, it comes mainly from the pseudo-intellectual, but it can destroy an aspiring author's confidence and a possible career. To such ill-informed opinion I urge you to turn a deaf ear, even though I am the first to concede that a totally unimaginative person would be more successful in another sphere (which they would be likely to seek anyway).

I am one who never attended writing classes, but I did have the advantage of four years on that long-established up-market monthly, *Woman's Journal*, first as secretary to its distinguished editor, then advancing to editorial work and journalism. During those years 'The Journal' was linked with three other publications, two women's weeklies and a highly regarded literary monthly called *Argosy*, devoted entirely to the best in short stories.

Part of my training was in the field of fiction; learning what was required for the respective magazines; what was publishable and what was not; what readers would enjoy and what they would not (and why); reading submitted manuscripts, criticising them, reporting to an exacting fiction editor and facing the music if my judgement proved to be wrong.

I also sub-edited fiction, from short stories to serials, including the works of many established authors. This taught me the value of economy and how judiciously to cut superfluous material. This was my training ground but, had I realised it, it was really my prep school. Searching for and editing publishable stories was a far cry from actually writing them. The toughest part came later; the slogging, stimulating, heart-breaking, challenging job of freelance authorship which, I quickly realised, is an entirely different skill from journalism or editing. Only then – writing, writing, writing – did my learning really begin.

The first salutory lesson was that authorship, like any creative work individually undertaken, is a lonely job. After the stimulation and team work of a busy editorial office, working in isolation demanded self-discipline. Domesticity vied with nostalgia for Fleet Street, at that time the heart of newspaper and magazine publishing, but I soon realised that freelancing offered the biggest plum of all – freedom to work in my own time, to be rid of commuting and its time-wasting hours, to combine writing with married life, and so to fulfil my ambition to become an author. To anyone who shares that ambition, solitude is something to seize with gratitude. It is another signpost to be well heeded.

So if you are finding the going hard, just remember that I (and others) have been there too. And if creative writing classes and textbooks help you, as they can, don't listen to those who have no faith in them. In particular, don't listen to those – usually relations, but often so-called friends – who regard your writing as nothing but a hobby, and not much of a one at that. ('When are you going to look for a proper job? You'll never make money, scribbling!')

Equally, don't pay too much heed, tempting as it may be, to those who say they have always known you were a born writer. Fulsome praise can be as damaging as derision, persuading you that any failure you may experience must be the fault of others, never of yourself.

Conquering discouragement

I have great respect for tutors in the field of creative writing when it comes to discussing and dissecting writing techniques, but it is only when an author is alone with his pen and a stack of blank paper that his heart and his imagination will take over. If urged in another direction by someone else, imagination can retreat, partly through self-consciousness but also through the fear of not matching up to a tutor's expectations or to the success of fellow students. And if the criticism of one's peers is involved, this sensitivity can be intensified. That is why I doubt the wisdom of students' efforts being read aloud in class, and when fellow aspirants are allowed to form a jury their verdict can be, at best, unreliable and, at worst, damaging.

I once witnessed a writers' circle meeting when competition entries were being read aloud and then voted on by members. Never having belonged to a writers' circle, I was shocked to learn that such a practice was indulged in. They had been asked to write a story about a chair. Inevitably, there were stories about Grandfather's chair (all too obviously cribbed from the old nursery song about his clock), about antique chairs, rocking chairs, children's high chairs, even an old kitchen chair which was actually supposed to be telling what little story there was.

But one entry featured something different – the electric chair, and the thoughts of the man condemned to it. It was so well written that not until the end did one realise what the chair actually was, or to where the man's journey of salvation was leading him. Even more clever was the note of hope throughout the tale. It was deeply moving and far from depressing. When it was unanimously awarded the lowest marking of all – 1 point – it was plain to me that the excellence of the writing, the originality of the idea, the deep compassion, and the skilful way in which it avoided any hint of despair, were totally unappreciated by the author's rivals.

I asked to be introduced to the writer and was not surprised to find her valiantly hiding disappointment. Convinced that her story deserved publication, I urged her to send it to one or two specific markets and was delighted, but again not surprised, when her story was eventually published. Whether the winning entry ever was – a twee tale about dear pussy's favourite chair – I very much doubt.

While it can sometimes be helpful to get an independent opinion on a piece of work, and even more helpful if you can get a professional one, I deplore the practice of exposing a beginner's work to the criticism of others equally inexperienced. Dorothea Brande, in her excellent book *Becoming a Writer*, includes a footnote for teachers in which she condemns the practice as pernicious and an ordeal which could throw sensitive writers off their stride and that when a beginner is judged in such a way, his or her critics seem eager to demonstrate that although they are not yet writing *quite* perfectly themselves, they are able to see all the flaws in a story which is read to them and 'fall upon it tooth and fang'. I saw it happen that night.

Every aspiring author will grow at his own pace, in his own time and in his own way, if his self-confidence is not undermined or even destroyed by criticism from unqualified sources, amongst which other aspiring authors can frequently figure. Criticism can and should be *con*structive, never *de*structive, as a writer will begin to discover when an editor begins to take an interest in his work and suggests ways in which to improve it. That is part of an editor's job, and to listen is part of a writer's.

Keep your own counsel

I strongly advocate the wisdom of never discussing your current piece of work with anyone. I myself have erred in this way, and regretted it. In one memorable instance, when asked by a fledgling author whom I had befriended, what the theme of my next novel was to be, I happily discussed it. I was about half way through the first draft, and enjoying it; a tale about the Owlers of Romney Marsh. She had never heard of that notorious gang of smugglers and enthusiastically asked for more, and more I foolishly revealed. I even outlined the basic plot, and was pleased by her appreciation of it. I even went a step further and introduced her to my agent. After that I never heard from her again.

Perhaps you have guessed the outcome, but I didn't even see it coming. She beat me to the post with a short novel set in the same place, at the same time, amongst the same notorious gang and with very familiar echoes; whilst my own book, of much greater length, had still far to go.

I knew nothing of this until hers was in print, by which time I could have been accused of plagiarism had mine then appeared. Plagiarism is a serious offence and can land an author in trouble. I had no choice but to withdraw a script which represented well over a year's work, and ask my publisher to wait for my next. I had neither the desire nor the inclination to reshape my story to avoid clashes with hers, nor would it have worked well had I done so. My enthusiasm and my book had been killed stone dead.

Fortunately, incidents like that are rare. Far more frequent are those when an author, in response to a genuine interest from others, has begun to talk about his or her current work, only to find that in the telling it begins to sound flat and dull, particularly when a listener's attitude confirms it. Pamela Frankau's

Pen to Paper offers a good example of this experience. She had the theme of her next novel 'safely tucked away in her head' after weeks of careful planning and even longer research, and went to a party feeling wildly happy because of it. Confiding the reason for her excitement to another guest, the woman immediately begged to hear all about it.

The author went ahead, only to find that with every word she spoke, it lost its magic; every character seemed cardboard, every situation contrived, and the reaction of her listener spoke volumes. In talking about it, the book became stillborn.

These instances are quoted only in warning, to urge you to guard your precious ideas. Always keep in mind that it is when a writer is alone with pen, paper, and an urgent desire to write what he or she *wants* to write, that the best work comes. Keep it right there before showing it to, or talking about it with, others.

Even when finished, there can be daunting discouragement. My own experience with *Dragonmede* was one. Read first by an editor newly employed by my UK publishers – a former magazine serial editor who had switched to the very different sphere of book publishing – it was condemned by her on the grounds that there were too many characters and that the whole plot therefore needed drastic cutting and reshaping.

'Remember,' she wrote, 'that no full-length should have more than six characters ...' and went on to suggest slashing out half the cast (including the central figure of a murderer vital to the plot) and consequently eliminating half the action and all conviction. I left her letter unanswered until, a month later, she wrote enquiring how far I had progressed with 'the very necessary reshaping', whereupon I sent her an outline of what would happen to the story were such alterations made, the whole thing falling apart.

I lacked the heart to tell her that she was viewing the novel in terms of a magazine serial, but from my own editorial experience I knew she was. Her very reference to a 'full-length', at that time a much-used editorial term for serials as distinct from short stories, revealed that she had not left the magazine world behind her. This was also confirmed by her demand for only six characters, which was then the convenient quota for serials because the limitations of instalments demanded that the cast should reappear in each instalment month by month or week by week. Drop them for longer, and 'out of sight out of mind' could well make readers forget them and the parts they originally played. I did venture to point out that a novel, unlimited by such space restriction, has a vast canvas with matching scope for characterization; that characters can enter and exit and enter again without any need for re-introduction because the reader has the entire volume in hand. She was unconvinced and replied that she would talk the whole thing over with me on her return from holiday.

In her absence my agent's American counterpart sold the US Hardback Rights to a leading New York publisher without any change being asked for. It also won a United States Literary Guild Alternate Selection, an Exclusive Selection of the Doubleday Book Club, more book club selections in Europe, Australia, Scandinavia and the UK, on top of big paperback auctions in America, and continuous worldwide paperback publication for several years. Its life was long and lucrative. Even now, royalties arrive unexpectedly from various corners of the globe. In all, its life span covers more than twenty-five years.

So take heart and don't give up hope. Your critics may not always be right.

But if you feel they may be, even slightly, take heed.

The author's greatest ally

It isn't surprising that sensitive writers retreat when hurt by harsh or unmerited criticism, but if they retreat with the intention of ploughing their own furrow and sticking to it, that is all to the good. Not only do the heart and mind take over when no one is looking over one's shoulder, the subconscious takes over too.

And so we come to another signpost – the author's greatest friend, the subconscious mind. In the first volume of this book I used the perfectionist's preference for 'unconscious', although there are arguments for and against. This time I yield to the majority choice of 'subconscious'. By whatever name, this hard-working mental tool assists us even when our conscious mind is occupied with day-to-day demands. It even works when sleeping. To wake in the night, suddenly aware of a solution to a tricky situation, an elusive sentence, or a telling title, is a common experience amongst authors. That is why a jotting pad and pencil at a writer's bedside are virtually essential. I recommend them to all beginners.

A great deal more can be done to slay the dragon of discouragement. If, for instance, you are attending creative writing classes but seem unable to produce what your tutor is looking for while other students do so with apparent ease, don't throw it all away in despair or, even worse, decide to give up.

Tutors of writing can be of tremendous value to beginners by offering inspiration and encouragement, by teaching basic fiction structures, by recommending worthwhile reading, and by concentrating on grammar, composition, syntax and style, but at that stage some aspiring writers decide that they must lack what it takes because their marks are declining and their tutor has begun to suggest, in all kindness, that perhaps they have not been really listening or concentrating. I have even heard of tutors suggesting that the student should try some other art form (and writing *is* an art form, no matter how non-writers may classify it). Or perhaps the tutor seems genuinely disappointed, which makes the tyro feel guilty and, even worse, a failure – and a sense of failure is the monster that I want to help you to overcome.

The first step is to remember that teachers in any creative field are not oracles. However sincere their intentions and however greatly your classmates may seem to please them, remember that a tutor's selection of exemplary fiction will often be chosen according to personal taste. He may well have excellent judgement, but it is still his individual choice. If it happens to be the student's too, well and good. In studying style and approach and every other aspect of the chosen model, an aspiring author will learn a lot but, again, must beware of slavish imitation. To model your style and approach on that of another can retard your development as an author. You must speak with your own voice.

Vaulting the hurdles

The initial difficulties which beset most new writers are by no means insurmountable unless believed to be. The mere fact that you *want* to write can help to overcome them.

Very common is the difficulty of actually making a start. More often than not this is caused by fear – fear of being unable to express yourself, fear of the pristine page, fear of marring it with bad prose, fear of it remaining in its pristine state after a long and fruitless session spent in staring at a blank sheet of paper which refuses to be filled.

It is a dreadful feeling, but you are not unique in experiencing it and there is a practical way of dealing with it.

It has been said that the bravest thing a writer can do is to put down the first word, but this is precisely what you *must* do and you don't have to have an idea in your head to do it. Stop seaching frantically for an opening or for some arresting phrase that will usher in more at pellmell speed; stop beating your brains for the right word because at this stage any word will do. One word leads to another, slowly and perhaps painfully but gathering momentum. Write anything and follow where the words lead. Tear them up if you want to, but if so you *must start again immediately.*

It is rather like the old party game of Consequences, writing down a sentence and then passing it to someone else to add another, except that in this instance the game is played solo, with the result that some sequence does form and in the process the once pristine page becomes ink-covered, proving that you *can* put your mind to it, you *can* compose sentences and paragraphs and chapters. I recommend this exercise whenever you experience self-doubt. You will be surprised by what comes out of it, and more particularly by the way it sparks ideas. Once ideas begin to form, the next page will begin to show purpose and direction.

Another difficulty, and a frightening one, can be the inability to follow up success. You have sold your first short story or novel and the publisher has asked for another, but your mind goes blank. Enter self-doubt again, then panic, then the conviction that you are a 'one-off' author, incapable of producing more. You force yourself, but produce very inferior stuff which persuades you that your conviction is justified. You have a rejected script to prove it, and when it continues to be rejected you withdraw from your writers' circle or literary group because you feel that everyone is waiting to hear of your next success. Failure embarrasses and even humiliates you, so you retreat.

This psychological problem is harder to deal with than the earlier one because no amount of hammered out words come to your rescue. There is only one thing to do – stop hammering, and stop asking yourself whether your one solitary success can only have been a flash in the pan. Look back on your achievement instead and acknowledge that you would never have accomplished that much if you lacked ability. Proof that you *can* write is there, staring you in the face.

So why can't you repeat it? The answer is simple. You are pushing yourself too hard; you are in too much of a hurry, too impatient, too anxious. You must relax and renew your acquaintanceship with reading, which you have almost certainly neglected while striving to follow up one success with another as quickly as possible.

That highly respected author and critic, Thomas Hinde, once remarked to me that 'if a writer isn't writing it's because he isn't reading'. He was right. So this is the time when instead of writing, writing, writing you must start reading, reading, reading. Not to copy, but to absorb.

Steep yourself in the works of others, but not necessarily of the genre you are specifically aiming for because the danger would, again, be that of unconscious mimicry. It is the easiest thing in the world, almost inevitable, that when you have finished reading a particular author whose writing absorbs you, you will, quite unawares, start aping their style – and that style is almost sure to be wrong for you, because you are a different writer, a different person with a different voice. Hence the need to steep yourself in a wide and varied range of literature, absorbing the *feel* of words just as, when listening to good music, you absorb the ebb and flow of sound.

The value of reading other people's books cannot be over-stressed. You get a sort of literary feed-back, stirring your own creativity. When that happens, the need to express yourself will become insistent – but don't be in a hurry. I have read many a hopeful author's story which has been dashed off too speedily, thereby ruining it.

I know one particular person who complains that her novels are rejected because publishers and agents misjudge them. She also prides herself on the speed at which she reads, and samples of her unsold stories prove them to have been written in the same way. It often happens that a too-speedy reader will be a too-speedy writer, and that brings me to the final signpost – the way to read, and the way to extract the utmost help from it.

Reading twice over

You will find, as you develop as a writer, that you read everything with a far more critical eye than you would if you were not one. You will also listen, in the same way, to every line of dialogue in a radio or television play. This is good, this is as it should be, though I sometimes infuriate my husband by saying aloud the next line of dialogue before the actor does (this is easy with predictable dialogue; not so easy if well written) but as far as reading is concerned I read, twice over, anything I have particularly enjoyed. In time you may well find yourself doing the same because you will no longer read as a library borrower dipping into the book merely for entertainment or relaxation.

If you fear that a lot of enjoyment will go out of reading once you cease to be uncritical, try my method – which, I am sure, is likely to be that of many another author. First read a book just as you would normally, in a relaxed and receptive frame of mind. You are sure to do this with authors whom you enjoy and you will also do it with an author whom you are reading for the first time but whose book, if you don't like it, you will probably put aside (though as your own writing skill develops you will become more analytical in seeking the reasons for your dislike).

Now read the book again, but with a different approach. This time you are going to find out just why you enjoy this particular author, or why you feel he or she didn't come up to scratch this time. Pay attention to the construction of the novel, the way in which problems are handled, the way in which one situation leads to another or grows out of another; pay special attention to the time factor and how the author moves his cast from place to place or from scene to scene without interrupting the flow or the rhythm of the story, and pay equal attention to the characters, to their behaviour and their dialogue and the skilful way in which they are portrayed – because it is the characters who bring stories to life.

It may help, in your analysis, if you sketch an outline of the book or, if you prefer merely to summarize, jot down questions and answers. Why did you enjoy it so much? Was it due to the action or to the characterization, to the setting or to the subtlety of atmosphere, to the pace and style? Then examine those things more closely, studying the opening and closing of chapters and the way in which the curtain rose and fell as scene followed scene before its final descent.

If you fear that this analytical approach will spoil the novel for you, or that it will distance you from the book or stale the memory of it, you are in for a surprise. You will feel closer to it than before, as if in some way you have taken part in its construction. And how much you will have learned during this critical process! So much that you cannot wait to take up your pen and face that stack of blank paper.

So now – let's do just that.

2. Creating a Story

Getting started

Popular fiction has many faces and many names: Crime, Thriller, Mystery, Romance, Suspense, Espionage, Western, Gothic, Romantic-Suspense, Historical, Science Fiction, Fantasy, Horror, Humour, Occult – and now Erotica, dubbed by some as the name publishers use to make porn sound respectable.

The categories are seemingly endless, but all – except perhaps the last, which has its own rules – have the same basic requirements; good characterization, a good plot, and the author's genuine enthusiasm for whatever genre he or she is aiming for. Sincerity is vital. Any story written tongue-in-cheek will be spotted at once by experienced editors and publishers. A work of fiction must be written because the author *wants* to write it, because he cannot rest until he does, because even if it is rejected and continues to be, that rejection will become a challenge and a challenge stimulates a mind which is intent on achieving a particular goal.

So after initial and often bitter disappointment, the author with a passionate urge to write will put a rejected novel out of sight and begin another. The chances are that he will have already started something else without waiting for a verdict on the first, and when he returns to the rejected one after completing the second he will find that the whole thing will be seen in better perspective and with a keener and more critical eye.

However strong the temptation, I urge every aspiring author never to make the mistake of discarding a rejected manuscript in a mood of self-disgust or even greater self-doubt, nor of immediately submitting it to another publisher without first re-reading it to assess whether its rejection was justified, and for what reason. The chances that unsuspected flaws will now leap from the page are high, especially if the script has been put away for a prolonged period.

There is no need for one rejection, or even more, to make you abandon hope. Stories of books being published after a chain of rejections are numerous. A notable one is that of James Hilton's *Goodbye, Mr Chips*, turned down by fourteen book publishers until an American magazine published it as a complete 'one shot' (a compact supplement at the end of the issue). It proved so popular that British book publishers then competed for the volume rights, and we all know what heights of success it achieved after that.

In many cases, books published after a chain of rejections are likely to have been rewritten and reshaped, often at the suggestion of a publisher's editor but sometimes after the author has had the good sense to accept the *challenge* of rejection, and to learn from it.

Another important thing to realise is that there is nothing personal about a rejection. 'Publishers don't seem to *like* me!' wailed an unsuccessful author I met. Despite my pointing out that no publisher or editor could have any personal prejudice against someone they did not know, she remained unconvinced that a script could be rejected for one of many reasons – because others of a similar genre happened to be in the stockpile (a reason unlikely to apply to specific category lists in which a publisher may specialize, such as crime), or because, for the moment, they were not publishing any more novels for economic reasons, or because it was the type of book they never published anyway, as the author could have discovered by studying library shelves or buying a copy of *Writers' & Artists' Yearbook* or *The Writer's Handbook* and turning to publishers' listings. There can be a dozen reasons for rejection, and none of them personal.

Once an author begins to believe that rejection is due to personal prejudice, a red light should flash. If he allows such an idea to persist he may be his own worst enemy.

Three vital ingredients

In addition to enthusiasm for his story, an author needs the two other essentials referred to earlier – good characterization and a good plot. These three requirements are predominant in all types of popular fiction because the aim is the same – to tell a story with a beginning, a middle, and an end. Variations (the individual demands of background, time, place, theme and genre) will all develop from there. Remember that the construction of a romantic novel or a crime novel or any other work of fiction differs from other categories only within its particular parameters.

But *how* to start? How to create that plot and those believeable characters?

Which comes first – plotting or characterization?

There is a common belief that the first step in writing fiction is to draw up a plot, and the second is simply to slot in some characters. Easy, you think, so you draw one up and devise situation after situation and development after development and you're off and away.

But are you? Think again. Do you really know the people whom you expect to fit so easily into your preconceived plan? How do they think, feel, react? Where do they come from? How have they been brought up? What influences have moulded their characters? Are they really the type of people to willingly dance to your tune? Wouldn't they prefer to dance to one of their own? And wouldn't they, being human, do precisely that, tangling the threads of your plot and leaving you stranded or at least hopelessly muddled?

To me, slotting characters into a ready-made plot would be like pinning cardboard figures on a map, and there is certainly a danger that a story so contrived would be unconvincing.

I am sure Humbert Wolfe was speaking from experience when he said that in good fiction one couldn't just rig up a plot and push the characters in afterwards; that the plot – the *story* – could only arise from the characters themselves. Somerset Maugham said the same thing, and historian Edward Gibbon endorsed it when saying that history is little more than a register of the crimes, follies and misfortunes of mankind. Pick up any newspaper and I think you'll agree that all three were right.

It is *people* who create plots; *people* who hold hostages to ransom, dethrone kings, kidnap children, intrigue politically, commit murder and rape and robbery; hold wives, husbands, parents, children and lovers in emotional bondage – or conversely (and omitted from Gibbon's list) achieve great things, commit acts of heroism and many romantic and unselfish deeds. Of such stuff and from such people are stories made.

Look back on your own life. How much of it have you been personally responsible for? How many decisions have you made and stuck to because you felt they were right, irrespective of other people's opinions? How many things have you deliberately decided to do, and what were the results? And how often have you said, 'If only I had done this . . . or that . . .' and then tried to visualise the outcome either way, making comparisons with your actual choice?

It is an undeniable fact that most people, intentionally or unintentionally, are responsible for many events in their lives. Not every twist and turn can be attributed solely to fate. We make choices, sometimes wisely and sometimes foolishly, but we make them all the same. Within our limitations and within the circumstances into which we were born we are responsible for a large part of our destinies, and as a result many of us overcome our limitations and our circumstances. So, too, do fictional characters. If you live with them, letting them simmer in your mind until you really *know* them, you will understand them, empathise with them, and give them their heads. You will then find that the claim of many authors that 'their characters take over' is not far from the truth.

The basic story idea will be yours, but the development and action come from the characters. That action must always be in keeping with their natures, since it is from their natures that it springs. So even when your hands are in control you must allow your characters to share the reins, otherwise they will pull against you and your story will run into difficulties. You must continuously ask yourself such questions as: 'Would he *do* such a thing?' 'Would a woman such as *she* be happy and at ease in such a situation?' 'Would such a couple behave that way?' 'Would such behaviour be *natural* in such a man?'

But though my personal belief is that characters come first, Elizabeth Jane Howard is quoted as stating categorically that theme is the first step. Far be it from me to take issue with so distinguished a writer but, like many, I find the term 'theme' somewhat vague, with shadowy elements waiting to be brought to life by the characters. If, for instance, you decide on nepotism as a theme, it inevitably suggests a family-run business with resentment and jealousy among employees. Without such essential characters waiting to demonstrate such emotions and to take action as a result, the story will be slow in getting off the ground.

The growth of a story

Many writers are familiar with the classic example of the need to know your characters first, which appears in Pamela Frankau's book *Pen to Paper*, but it is worth repeating because it is quoted from her personal experience.

When teaching English at a Post-Hostilities School of Army Education, she suggested one day that the class should write a short story. Asking where they would begin and what they would look for first, she received the united answer of, 'Plot!' Characters, they declared, could then follow, so it was agreed that she should set the plot and they would provide the characters.

The plot concerned a murderer who invited his two victims to dinner. His chosen method of killing was to screw down the dining room ceiling on top of them, crushing them to death, but at the last minute the victims were to be saved by the floor collapsing and dropping them a short distance into a cellar, out of harm's way.

The students accepted the plot unanimously and then set to work to produce the main character – the murderer. They gave the matter a great deal of thought and as they created him she listed the details on the blackboard. They chose to make him a civil servant and so, to their way of thinking, he had to be mousey and middle aged – and of course he had a mousey little middle aged wife. He did his job adequately, was never late for the office, caught the same commuter trains morning and evening, drove neither a car nor a motor-bike. He liked gardening, took his seaside holiday at the same place every year, was practically teetotal, a bad sailor, and paid his bills regularly. He was not much of a reader, certainly not of novels or poetry. A nice enough guy, in his way. Rather shy, with an inability to make close friends but always pleasant and well-mannered.

On the blackboard he was a complete and believable character. Then came the task of fitting him into the plot. She summed him up. A nice, timid, unadventurous chap; fond of routine and peace; no particular discontent; no hobbies except his garden; no mechanical knowledge, no special skills. The temperature began to drop, so she pressed on. Would he, not even a car driver or the owner of a motor-bike, be of a sufficiently mechanical turn of mind to devise a screw-down ceiling in order to commit this murder? And who were the enemies of this mild, dutiful, garden-loving man? Where were his motives? At a stroke, the plot collapsed. So, we are back to my golden rule. Get your characters first, and from them will come your plot *provided that you have taken the trouble to get to know them well.* This means living with them, letting them take over your mind and occupy your thoughts, and never hurrying them. Never hurry anything or force anything when writing fiction or you will stumble later on. When the moment is ripe to put pen to paper or fingers to keyboard, you will know well enough because nothing will stop you. The characters will be hammering at your mind, along with situations and developments which have come to you as a result of getting to know them so well.

Another contributory factor is that they are creatures of your own creation, born from your own imagination, and you can foster their development by exercising it more. As an example, let's start by taking the mild, garden-loving man created by those long-ago students and see what developments can result from the use of imagination.

Variations on a theme

Let's take a man with similar characteristics – we'll make him a retired schoolmaster and call him Horace – and consider how one of his nature *would* commit murder, and whom he would want to kill.

Since he has no enemies and is a quiet, reserved man without friends, wouldn't his life be bound up in his wife? And haven't the mildest of men been driven to murder throughout the course of history? One can see this meek, dutiful, routine-minded man simmering slowly to boiling point over a long period of time, bottling up resentment against his wife for imprisoning him in monotony, feeling cheated by her for not remaining the desirable woman he had once found her and quite unaware that *he* has ceased to be desirable to *her*. . .

In such a man, resentments could also be fanned by the success of working colleagues who have outstripped him, successively cheating him out of the headmastership he has always coveted and who apparently have all that he would regard as the trappings of success – a better house, a bigger garden, holidays abroad instead of annually at Skegness tied to his wife's skirts – but the murder poor Horace would commit would be too unimaginative to demand any James Bond stunts; more likely it would be a quiet, slow kind of murder, full of the surprising cunning that quiet, slow people can sometimes reveal.

And it could be the obvious one which any writer, given such a character, might make the first choice. Since the man is a keen gardener he could have access to weedkiller, the purchase of which is legal and would therefore arouse neither comment nor curiosity, especially at the local garden centre where he is known as a regular customer. He would also know, as all gardeners do, that certain weedkillers contain arsenic and, being intelligent enough to hold down his job adequately, he would be sufficiently intelligent to check on the effects of arsenic on the human body, using the reference room of his local library because he would not be so unwise as to buy books on poisons and keep them on his bookshelves or hidden somewhere in the house.

He would therefore be aware that arsenic is odourless and virtually tasteless, especially if administered in small doses over a period of time – in, say, the nice cup of tea he takes to his wife first thing every morning (the dear, devoted husband that he is). 'Four lumps as usual, Ethel dear. That sweet tooth of yours'll be the death of you yet!' I can see this quiet, gentle man enjoying that little joke and his wife not getting it at all.

And he would not make a special visit to the library to do his checking. Being a man of routine, he would do it when returning books for himself and his wife, as he has done every week throughout their marriage, and if he came back a little later than usual one evening he could easily make the excuse that he had had difficulty, this time, in finding the nice romantic novel she was wanting by her favourite romance author – and no excuse might even be necessary because the dull, mousey little woman has probably fallen asleep in front of the telly and not even missed him.

But since poison is known to be mainly a woman's instrument, another murder method could be invented for such a man. He could go berserk and kill his wife with an axe or carving knife, exploding after years of pent-up and slowly corroding hatred – this would be dramatic but not as suspenseful as a cunning, quietly thought-out murder, because a crime of such violence could not be covered up nor appear to be death by natural causes. It would also focus suspicion on him, however hard he tried to make out that a killer had broken in, whereas a record of stomach disorders and bouts of sickness over a period of time could establish a pattern of ill health and scarcely arouse comment since he had unfailingly called the doctor every time his wife had 'one of her bilious attacks'.

So how will he go about it and will-he-won't-he get away with it? How will the truth be discovered and bring him to justice? That is the exercise you must now work on, bearing in mind that if you want your story to be convincing, rather than contrived, all his actions must stem from his basic character.

Finding alternatives

The foregoing random thoughts restrict the tale to the crime category, but this retired schoolmaster and his wife offer other possibilities, bringing us to exercise number two – taking them into another category.

Let's see them as a typical Darby and Joan, celebrating their Golden or Diamond Wedding, a situation which could switch them into the sphere of romance, which is by no means confined to boy-meets-girl. We have now changed routes and landed in the world of sentiment, the old couple's love story ready to be relived with all its problems and its passions, its triumphs and disasters. This means that the personality and character of the wife must be developed as vividly as the husband's because she will have as great a part to play. It also means that the story can be written from either viewpoint.

Alternatively, still in the world of sentiment but not writing in retrospect, we can enter into the family celebration with the children and grandchildren who have come from far and near. However, this merely sets the scene. What of the plot? What of developments? In this category of fiction the theme must be wholly emotional and, again, this will be dictated by the characters themselves, by the depth of family affection, by filial devotion or lack of it, by jealousies and loves, even by hopes and dreams.

In yet another step we can move into the field of 'straight' magazine fiction, aiming for a market which publishes stories of social significance or psychological interest. We can write it from the angle of the wife who, after fifty years of silent and dutiful devotion, is goaded into tearing the blinkers from her husband's eyes by revealing her long suppressed feelings of resentment, frustration, and regret because she remained loyal to him and to their growing family and resisted the temptation to run away with another man – and now it is too late. Do her smouldering thoughts ignite to the pitch where she strikes back? If so, how? And what is the outcome?

Such a situation has boundless possibilities. It could be psychologically chilling or even funny if all she could do to celebrate the occasion was to hit him over the head with a flower pot. Or, for a sinister twist, how about something much heavier? Promptly, your story-telling mind is asking, 'And what happened then?', 'How would such a woman *then* behave?'

Or how about writing it from their family's viewpoint? Let's imagine the kind of children and grandchildren this aging couple would have and the way in which they themselves, in contrast, had been brought up, and immediately we have double generation gaps and triple social standards. A moving and even disturbing picture of that family reunion could then be built up, with the interplay of family misunderstandings, the inability of different generations to see eye to eye or to enjoy the same things, and the gradual surfacing of emotional undercurrents.

Such a story could be tragi-comic or sad, or given a happy ending with the intolerance of the young slowly evaporating as they realise that their grandparents are more understanding and more likeable than they expected and, after coming to the party unwillingly, they ask how soon they may come again.

Take any of these situations and develop them for yourself. That is exercise number two.

For exercise number three let's take Horace on his own and move him into yet another genre. This time we will make him an eccentric widower, living alone in a terraced London house, his only visitor being a cleaner-lady who 'does for him' daily and *she* knows better than to set foot in that attic where he spends all day and every day. Doing what? Nobody knows or cares until strange things begin to happen in this very respectable street; strange sounds emanate through that attic window, and then strange shapes are seen, and the cleaner-lady suddenly refuses to come back (or maybe she disappears?), then, one by one, fantastic creatures emerge and take over the street . . . and we are off into the science fiction category with Horace, the sci-fi fanatic, appalled (or excited) by the outcome of his secret experiments. (And, of course, for the Horror genre, you could make the creatures truly horrific, with horrific events and horrific results.)

For further variations on character and theme, we can take Horace into yet more categories; Mystery, Gothic, or even quirky Humour with some scheming lady taking advantage of his loneliness and leading him to the altar – at which point we give the tale an ironic twist by making him guess what she is after and thwarting her schemes by settling his money, before death, on his scattered children in order to avoid death duties.

Or, rather more romantically, we could imagine him as a Mr Chips type of character; endearing, lovable, possibly meeting again his first youthful love, now widowed.

And what about the realms of history? Decide on a famous or infamous character whose story fascinates you or sparks questions in your mind. For example, a king such as Richard III, portrayed as a monster by Shakespeare and more sympathetically by Josephine Tey in *Daughter of Time*; a man championed today by a vociferous society of supporters, but whose name remains associated with the murder of the princes in the Tower. Get a postcard or print of his famous portrait from the National Gallery and see what you detect in that patient, gentle, rather sad face. *You* may see none of those qualities in it, but only quiet, innocent-eyed cunning (the quality we first attributed to our retired schoolmaster). Ponder on it, and you may be off into the historical genre with yet another story about that allegedly notorious king.

The foregoing demonstrates how, from one imaginary character alone, a chain of ideas can spring. The permutations are endless so, for exercise number four, see how many more you can come up with about a man with Horace's characteristics, but bear in mind that each and every twist and every new variation of plot must not only involve him but emanate from him. As the central figure, he must be the pivot of the story. The main character is always at the centre of conflict, his problem the issue which runs through the tale and holds it together by giving it motivation.

The word 'conflict' does not necessarily mean the physical kind. It can be purely emotional. Conflicting ambitions, conflicting aims, conflicting loves, conflicting views, conflicting upbringings . . . whatever the type of conflict it must be *there*, centre stage.

It is also important to remember that no supporting characters must ever hog the limelight, so if you find that another character is threatening to take command, think again. You may have someone stronger who will lead you to a stronger plot, with Horace now relegated to a supporting role.

Remember, too, that each and every character must have an essential part to play. If they contribute nothing to the story's development, even in the smallest way, cut them out or they will clutter the scene and interrupt the action. Unnecessary characters are dead wood that no story can afford to carry.

But, staying with our imaginary Horace, remember too that in whatever category you wish to slot him, he won't fit into it unless his character changes fundamentally every time, and it won't do that unless you see him and know him thoroughly, so in whatever guise you dress him, leave him to grow in your mind. Don't hurry him. Don't rush anything. A story, like a plant, can grow only at its own pace and with the right nurturing.

And now, for exercise number five, replace this man with someone you have created wholly by yourself. This is important, not only to stretch your imagination but to help you to avoid the temptation, consciously or unconsciously, of stealing characters created by other writers – yes, I know that Jean Rhys did it in *Wide Sargasso Sea,* her brilliant and wholly imaginative story based on Mr Rochester's mad wife in *Jane Eyre*, but in no way is her novel a pastiche of Charlotte Brontë, nor does it encroach on the Bronte book in the slightest degree.

Wide Sargasso Sea is a totally independent story about a character who, to Charlotte Brontë, was no more than a lunatic locked up in an attic and branded, in the author's prejudiced mind, by her Creole blood; but this tragic character haunted Jean Rhys for years because it awakened her own memories of life in the West Indies as the daughter of a Creole mother who was herself one of the tragic Creole heiresses of the nineteenth century. Only if you can create something equally individual do you need no warnings from me.

So now pick up your pen and pad again and start inventing a characer uniquely your own. Try it out in various situations designed for various genres, as we did with Horace. When you find that the character fits into one more naturally than into another, you will have discovered the category you need to aim for.

3. Getting Ideas

Sources

You can find ideas anywhere and everywhere. In newspapers and magazines; in shops and trains; from people chattering in buses; from your own problems and those of others; from tryng to imagine, as I suggested earlier, what would have happened had you made a different choice at a certain time in your life; from political crises; from politicians' slanging matches; from a line of dialogue in film or play; from ancient houses and unfamiliar backgrounds; from people and places and even from things.

For instance, what does a piece of shattered china suggest to you? A clumsy visitor, a burglary, a fraught wife venting her frustration, a child trying to please its mother by doing the washing up, a shopper accidentally dislodging a counter display and being pounced on by the proprietor?

The world is full of ideas, if you look for them. You can even turn up basic plots in Georges Polti's *The Thirty-Six Dramatic Situations* which contains, in embryo, almost every book or play ever written – but keeping your eyes and ears open and giving your imagination free rein can serve you better. Do this on your way to or from work, when lunching in snack bars, queueing for buses or sitting in traffic jams. Study your fellow passengers; focus your mind on one in particular and try to imagine his or her background, occupation, likes and dislikes. What sort of a house or flat do they live in and in what sort of neighbourhood or street? Do they live alone or with boyfriend or girlfriend? Is the relationship temporary or has it achieved the permanent-sounding term of 'partnership'? Or are they married; have they children?

Study their facial expression; is it gentle, pugnacious, wistful, petulant, kindly, humorous, peevish or good-natured? What are they thinking about as they sit staring idly into space?

Your answers may well be very wide of the mark, but gradually you will have your own picture of them and can start

27

weaving your story. Imagine someone waiting for them when they reach their destination. Will they rush to meet each other or merely exchange a peck on the cheek? If only the latter, why? Is it a kiss of indifference from a married partner who has come only from a sense of duty, or is it a kiss of shyness because they don't know each other intimately yet? So what lies ahead? Give your imagination free rein; let it come up with whatever notion it fancies. By the time you reach your own destination it will be going full blast.

Ideas can also come from sayings or from song titles, from poetry remembered from childhood, from proverbs and quotations, and from chance remarks. My novel, *The Mating Dance*, sprang from a comment of David Attenborough's during one of his TV documentaries, and another made to me many years earlier by an actor, Nigel Patrick. Nigel's parents had been professional actors and I had never forgotten him telling me, as we foot-slogged between theatrical agencies around Shaftesbury Avenue and the Charing Cross Road one long-ago morning during my unsuccessful theatrical days, that he had actually been born in a dressing room. His mother had continued to perform right up to the time of his birth (luckily it was a period piece and required flowing robes) and when he decided to arrive in a hurry her theatrical skip had been used as a cradle.

(At this point I feel I should stress that when needing to demonstrate how to handle a specific writing problem, I will either make up a simple illustration or quote from my own published work. I can then speak from personal experience and explain the intention behind it with greater authority. Exceptions will occur when I wish to pay tribute to a particular writer's ingenuity or skill.)

So how were the remarks of David Attenborough and Nigel Patrick linked, and how did they spark a novel set in the Victorian theatreworld?

'This is their mating dance,' said David Attenborough as two exotic birds weaved and pranced, and 'What a title for a book!' I said to my husband. I let the title simmer until, over a period of months, the background suggested itself. The word 'dance' indicated a frequent change of partner, and frequent change suggested promiscuity, and *that* suggested a world where it was commonplace. Promiscuity now being openly indulged, another period was essential. I chose the Victorian, in which immorality was taboo in respectable circles, but not in the theatrical world. Then I recalled Nigel Patrick's story and there I was, in a theatrical dressing room.

The opening setting was ready to hand, but not the characters. All I could see was the newborn child lying in a battered theatrical skip; no one else, not even the mother. I knew she was an actress, but no more than that because she stubbornly refused to come to life. I therefore came to an abrupt halt. Finally, I abandoned the idea of a child being born, but retained the setting. Even then, and despite laborious mental searching, I could people that dressing room with nothing more than a glamorous leading lady, glitter, romance, gushing admirers, adoring Stagedoor Johnnies, champagne, the popping of corks, ogling and laughter and artificiality.

But that wasn't what I wanted. It was trite. The opening had to be more down to earth, more realistic and more dramatic. Finally despairing I abandoned it, but the setting refused to let me go. So did the newborn child. For weeks my mind kept advancing and retreating, haunting the place, seeing nothing but a picture of an actress giving birth after the curtain had fallen, an actress without face or form. Something was wrong.

Questions began to plague me. How soon would she be acting again and who would take her place in the meantime? If she had continued to perform right up to the moment of her child's birth, plainly she had no understudy, so that character was ruled out. I had reached a dead end when the first really constructive answer hit me. *It was not the leading lady who gave birth, but another woman, one who would always be in the dressing room with her – her dresser.*

Promptly, I was asking how the leading lady would react to such an inconvenient event and *then* things began to fall into place, and so did the necessary characters for my opening scene. Beyond that I could visualise nothing. I made no outline. I put pen to paper and sought the first line, letting it lead me where it willed. My first paragraph flowed:

> I was literally born to the smell of greasepaint, inhaling it with my first breath in the dressing room of the great Bernadette Boswell during a matinee on June 16, 1880, an indiscretion for which she never wholly forgave my mother. It was not the privilege of dressers to give birth in star dressing rooms, leaving the leading lady unbuttoned all the way down

the back and the call-boy shouting 'Beginners, please!' outside the door.

Following a mere thread I had established the place, the period, the time of day, the characters who were to start the story and relevant facts about each. I had written what is known as a narrative hook (on which I will enlarge in Chapter 9), an opening paragraph designed to lead, as all opening paragraphs should, to the question of what happened next.

I had no idea. I was an onlooker, watching the characters, and because they had been growing in my mind I knew that the leading lady was an overbearing woman who would consider such an event not only inconvenient but outrageous. I knew she would therefore go rushing to the wings, shouting for help, not for her dresser, but for herself, her only thought being that someone had to button her up, her selfishness clearly indicating her inability to forgive (a characteristic which would plainly increase as the novel grew, and so influence developments). So another character had to enter, preferably without knocking for admission. That person's identity was obvious.

Married couples often share dressing rooms, or have communicating ones, so the entry of the great Bernadette's husband was inevitable. In he came, hurrying to see what was wrong and finding the poor dresser in a mighty predicament. And of course one question about the dresser hit me. Why was she working so near her time? Surely the average husband, however poor, wouldn't let her? Answer: she had no husband so the lack of money, and the child's illegitimacy, became important to the story.

This is how plots spring from characters. Their actions and reactions spark situations and their problems create others.

But that is just one example. Let's take another, not from a title or a quotation this time, but from a remark I actually overheard in a New York restaurant on my first visit very many years ago. Two women were sitting at the next table, close enough for their conversation to be unavoidably overheard. I have never forgotten it.

'And how's Mary-Lou?' asked one.

'Oh, she's fine,' said the other. 'She's just made her first marriage.'

Perhaps it was naïve of me to find the remark astonishing. In those days America had the highest divorce rate in the world, so the lack of reaction from the woman's companion, other than mild interest, should also not have surprised me.

'That so?' said she. 'A good one?'

'Good enough, I guess.'

Good enough to go on with? Good enough until she finds another? Good enough until she does better for herself? Was that what the mother actually meant?

This immediately sparked the idea for a short story about an ambitious woman who disapproved of her daughter's marriage to a man considered (by ambitious Mama) to be reasonably acceptable socially but rather less so financially; a good enough stop-gap, but no more. By the time I returned to England the story was alive in my head; the story of a scheming mother with an ugly-duckling daughter married off to a passable man while Mama remained hopeful that someone more acceptable would turn up to be husband number two.

With maturity, the daughter blossomed and Mama's hopes soared. With calculated cunning the woman cast her net, entertaining on a scale she could not afford, manipulating introductions to a higher social scale and focusing on successful men – finally on a thrice-divorced and wealthy financier who would make a highly acceptable son-in-law (with all that lovely name-dropping ahead!). She also expended time and energy in determinedly breaking up her daughter's marriage.

All went according to plan. The desired divorce went through and to her mother's satisfaction the girl willingly let the eminent gentleman squire her around. She was seen everywhere in his chauffeur-driven Rolls which he, obsessed, insisted she should use when shopping. Much elated, scheming Mama's name-dropping began, coupled with unashamed bragging about the identity of her new son-in-law-to-be until, to her horror, the daughter eloped with a man even poorer and less socially acceptable than the first – the chauffeur – leaving dear Mama not only financially embarrassed but socially embarrassed as well.

Put baldly, the plot was slight, but it lent itself well to a 3000-word short story and the characters were alive because they were vivid to me. I quote it only as an example of how chance remarks can give birth to ideas.

What about other sources? A newspaper item, perhaps. Let's take an imaginary one from a small town journal, and see what ideas it sparks.

MISSING WOMAN RETURNS AFTER
TWENTY-FIVE YEARS

Elspeth Marshall was twenty-three when she disappeared from her home in the village of Woodfield, leaving her husband – Joseph Marshall, proprietor of The White Horse – and a two-year-old daughter. Prolonged searching yielded no trace. Her disappearance coincided with a series of murders in the vicinity and the police were finally forced to conclude that she had been a victim. Her body was never found. Joseph Marsall remarried and continued to run The White Horse with his second wife. Three months ago he was killed in a car crash. Elspeth Marshall refuses to be interviewed.

Your imagination has much to feed on here. Where had Elspeth been for the last twenty-five years? Why had she gone? What had driven a young mother to leave her husband and child? How had she been living since then, and with whom? The newspaper gives no details other than the bare facts of her disappearance, so you can weave any imaginary pictures that appeal to you.

Start yet again by asking yourself questions. Has she returned because she has heard of her husband's death and thinks she can claim the profitable village pub? After all, the death of his first wife was never proved so wasn't his second marriage bigamous? Or has Elspeth returned because her daughter is now grown up and she hopes to make her understand her mother's actions and to be reunited with her? And, if so, how will the daughter react? She will now be twenty-seven and possibly married; she may well have left the village and, even if she has not, she probably has no recollection of her mother. All she knows is that she was abandoned by her at the age of two. Hardly someone to put out the welcome mat for.

Having answered these questions, and any others your imagination conjures up, decide on the angle from which you intend to start. How about that of the woman who is now, legally or otherwise, the 'official' Mrs Marshall? Would she refuse to be ousted from this profitable and comfortable inn which is not only her source of income but her home? Does she believe that possession *is* nine tenths of the law? Has Joseph Marshall left a will, or not? Does a legal wrangle ensue? And on whose side would the daughter be? Is the relationship between stepmother and stepdaughter strong, or shaky? A battle between three members of the same sex could certainly develop from this angle.

Or the story could go off on a different tack. The Elspeth Marshall who returns is rich and successful, proprietor of a prominent chain of boutiques selling way-out teenage gear. She was penniless when she disappeared, so from where did she get the money to launch such a business? Her surname is unchanged and there appears to be no man in her life. So how did her successful career get started and what brings her back to the quiet country village where the inhabitants are mainly middle-aged or elderly, its only attraction being the popularity of The White Horse for weekenders? Could it be the proximity of a rapidly growing town only a few miles distant? Does she feel, now her husband is really out of the way, that she can open a branch there, buy a house in her native village and expect to be accepted by the local inhabitants, many of whom have long, critical and suspicious memories and now wonder who engineered the car crash which so conveniently killed her husband?

With thought, this imaginary newspaper item can spark a variety of ideas. My personal choice would be to tell the story through the eyes of the daughter who, quietly and determinedly, probes for the truth about her mother's past and keeps silent about it until such time that she chooses. This approach could lead to bitterness or eventual understanding, but either way it would lead to conflict, that essential quality in all story-telling. Conflict would come from the daughter if she could not forgive her mother, and the daughter would also experience strong emotional conflict if, in forgiving her, she felt disloyal to her father. And there would be inevitable conflict between the first wife and the second in which the daughter could feel trapped.

Scenes of emotional conflict present great scope because emotion comes from the heart. All writing should come from the heart if it is to attract and hold the reader's interest.

You will have noticed that the news item I made up was short and of no world-wide or national interest. When scouring press columns for ideas it is wise to look for the buried paragraph, the seemingly unimportant, even the trivial. Never latch on to the latest sensation, or the biggest scandal, or any highly topical theme. If you do, you will almost certainly share the fate of dozens of other writers whose typescripts will boomerang back from editorial offices which have been innundated with stories based on the same sensation, a sensation already being flogged to death by the media and with which the public is rapidly becoming bored.

33

'But,' you may argue, 'lots of famous criminal cases and notorious scandals have been turned into novels.' True. Judith Rosner's *Looking for Mr Goodbar* is an example. Based on a tragic real life murder case in America, the book succeeded because it far excelled others based on the same tragedy (some of which were published, but eclipsed). However, the advice I give throughout this book is mainly for the inexperienced writer and unless you happen to be a natural genius (in which case you need no help from me) you would be wise to avoid competition with the many other writers who seize on the latest sensation.

The best use for ideas gleaned from press sources is for exercising the imagination, for getting the mental wheels turning, for releasing words on to paper, after which the real you will emerge, urging you to write to your own ideas.

Other sources

Some of the most creative ideas come from situations or characters which suddenly present themselves visually. To illustrate this I must again quote from personal experience.

My novel, *Dragonmede*, emerged from a picture which sprang to mind about two years before I started writing the book. As always with things springing from the unconscious, I have no idea where it came from, but I had a vivid mental picture of an Edwardian lady wearing a blue velvet costume trimmed with sable, and a splendid hat covered in matching blue. She carried a sable muff. Later, a child thrust herself into the picture, holding the woman's hand and skipping along happily. The woman was smiling down at her, indifferent to the fact that her own elegant skirts were sweeping the ground. That told me the child meant more to her than her fine clothes.

Mother and child lingered with me for months. The woman had long, tapering fingers which I could imagine hovering over a silver tea-stand and delicate porcelain. Later, that was replaced with a more vivid picture of the same hands dexterously dealing a pack of cards. This picture finally took hold of me, and so did a sudden question: could this fashionable lady run an exclusive card-playing salon, even a notorious one from which she would make a point of excluding her daughter as she grew up? Why not? I knew instinctively that she was warm-hearted, immoral by conventional standards, protective of, and ambitious for, her daughter.

After considering the best angle from which to write, I discarded several openings and left it to the daughter, now growing up, to tell their story.

And so I began, again with no outline and only the mother and daughter in mind. Instinctively again, I let the daughter's voice speak the opening lines.

By most standards my upbringing was scandalous, though it was a long time before the fact was brought home to me. As a child I accepted, without question, the bohemian, rather shameful but happy life I lived with my mother until I was old enough to realise that it was, to say the least, unconventional, and even then I continued to accept it because whatever her mode of living, her lack of morals, and her feckless attitude to money, my mother had the rare ability to make life rich and full and warm. She lived generously and she loved generously, and more than all she loved me.

Once a picture is vivid in your mind, it will seize you, hold you, and carry you forward. The more you write, the more visually you will see everything.

Such pictures can also linger with you from scenes actually witnessed. I remember seeing a laden young soldier on Waterloo Station. He was obviously home on leave and waiting for someone. His expression was tense, his restless pacing betrayed his feelings and his fears: she wasn't coming, she had stood him up or, worse, she had met with an accident. Only someone very much in love could display such tension. And then the girl came running, breathless, eager: his expression changed from anxiety to joy; wordlessly they met, wordlessly they clung. I still recall them because a whole story of young love was there, of hope, of joy after separation. A romantic ending, or a romantic beginning? I often wondered and I never made up a story about them. So why, as yet another exercise, don't you?

Witnessing a situation can be rewarding and, since it is people who create situations, such scenes provide a springboard for action. Imagine seeing a woman jumping into an Underground train as the doors are closing; she is wearing a flimsy summer skirt and the rush of air sucks it inward, trapping it, leaving her outside and dragging her with it. Such a situation presents mind-boggling possibilities. This is where you must tackle it with the old and tried method of question and answer.

How is she saved? By her skirt ripping at the crucial moment so that she falls on to the platform? But suppose it is winter and the cloth is tough? She will be saved even more convincingly then because she will be wearing a coat and the thick material will prevent the doors from closing completely, signalling to the driver that something is wrong. In the days when I travelled to work by Underground I saw many a commuter scramble aboard at the last minute by thrusting a handbag or folded newspaper in the aperture just before the doors met. They would promptly jerk open again. A strongly shod male foot was always useful, so isn't there a germ of an idea for a romantic encounter there . . . a gallant young man rushing to her aid?

But wider scope and deeper investigation is needed. Time and place have been established, but not why she steps on to the train so tardily. First you must know the type of person she is, because this will tell you why she is late. It will also give the story that much-needed motivation. Is she absent-minded and, if so, why? Is she merely a day-dreamer? Perhaps she is lazy, with a tendency to oversleep or dawdle when getting ready for work. Is she emotional, her mind occupied with a lovers' quarrel? Is she a worrier who broods over problems, say a difficult mother or a fretful child (immediate introduction of other characters), or is she merely suffering from a hangover after a late party which she now regrets? So what kind of woman is she to go to the kind of parties one regrets? Who took her there and why was she willing to go? Is she weak and easily influenced?

Over to you. I made her up so, like Elspeth Marshall in the imaginary news paragraph, I give her to you. Bring her to life; bring both women to life, and their stories with them.

Places and backgrounds

These can be potent sources for ideas. To me, the very atmosphere of Glencoe conjures up the massacre of the MacDonalds, and from this sprang an earlier novel, *Glenrannoch*.

In the same way, houses of all kinds can speak volumes. Empty houses, ancient houses, occupied houses; country houses and town houses; isolated cottages and ruined castles. Questions are promptly launched in my mind and I am instantly wondering who lived in such-and-such a place, who built it, how many people occupied it, when and for how long and, in the case of deserted buildings, why they were abandoned. *What happened there?* Many a horror story has grown out of houses made notorious by infamous crimes.

I recall seeing crime writer P D James in a TV series featuring prominent authors and their working methods. She was walking on Brownsea Island, asking herself who had built the house there, who had abandoned it, what made them leave. Into her mind, she said, crept shadowy people and there she planned to let them remain, to take their own shape and form until eventually she knew how they looked, behaved, reacted; the things they were likely to do or not do. From them the plot would develop.

The sources for ideas that I have mentioned here are but a few. You will discover more for yourself the more you write, for the more you write the more your ideas will flow.

Exercising the imagination

This chapter has been demonstrating not only how to get ideas, but how to develop them with judicious use of the imagination. There are other ways in which you can exercise this most valuable tool, without which the most brilliant plot can remain a mere skeleton. How you clothe its bones depends entirely on you. No two writers would do it the same way.

This was put to the test, some years ago, by an editor named Fothergill, who hit on the idea of circulating a basic plot amongst a number of authors to develop into a short story. The results were so different that, to prove his point, he published them in an anthology. Each author had clothed the skeleton according to his own imagination, but the interesting outcome was that all the stories were badly reviewed. 'Dull' was the general verdict, proving that a plot produced from a blue print, instead of from an individual author's imagination, can be uninspiring.

But the most vivid imagination can sometimes need exercising. Here are one or two ways in which to prod it.

(1)   Set yourself a problem; make it as difficult as possible. Then set a time limit in which to solve it; not too short and not too long. Too short would mean pressure and pressure

can cause panic and panic can make the imagination dry up. Too long can lead to a feeling that you have all the time in the world, and so to laziness. I suggest you give yourself two weeks in which to come to grips with it. Carry the problem in your mind wherever you go and let your imagination take over.

(2)   Take a rejected story out of its hiding place and look for its weakest character. Almost unfailingly there will be one less effective than the rest. See how you can strengthen it. See how the change affects the plot and how, by altering the *motivation* of that character, the story too changes course. You will find yourself rethinking and rewriting the whole thing and producing a much better and more saleable story.

(3)   Timing. If you are in the middle of a story and it drags, try changing its pace. Start at an earlier point, at an incident which you have mentioned only in passing or even in retrospect. You may have missed an opportunity for action, so go back and *start* there. If there is no such incident, create one. Either way, your imagination will get a tremendous spur and so will the pace of the story, bringing it alive.

Alternatively, look ahead. Perhaps you started the story too far back, so take a leap forward instead. This may present a surprising impetus and will almost certainly spark new ideas.

Telling the tale

When I am asked how I write a novel – a question which always seems to demand some magic formula in answer – I can only say, truthfully, that I tell myself the story as I go along but, before I begin to write, certain characters and certain scenes evolving *from* them have been simmering in my mind, sometimes for a long time, sometimes briefly. None of these scenes could have come about had I tried to pluck the characters out of thin air. Even snatches of their dialogue have come to me, sometimes forgotten but occasionally dredged up in their entirety. If you experience the same thing but doubt your memory, jot down the dialogue without delay. Also note down important bits of characterization which will help you, when you start writing, to see and hear your characters as vividly as when they first crept into your mind.

Because I see everything visually, writing a novel is, to me, rather like occupying a seat in the stalls and watching the whole drama unfold before me. That is what makes a novel come alive for me, though of course it is really the characters who do that. Characters obsess me and when I am actually writing I see them in action, hear them talking and, with a novelist's privilege, am allowed to know what they are thinking and feeling. At such moments comes the conviction that not only do *I* know *them*, but *they* know *me*.

But what of the short story? It's all very well, you say, to expand at length on the lengthiest form of fiction, but your job or your family or a dozen other things leave you no time to try your hand at a novel. Meanwhile, something short must be easy to knock off and easy to sell . . .

There is only one answer to that – turn to the next chapter.

4. The short story

A genre of its own

The difference between a novel and a short story is like that between a landscape painting and a thumbnail sketch. The novelist has a vast canvas on which to present not only the focal points, but a wealth of detail and many characters; the short story writer has space only for the focal points and rarely more than two main characters, one of whom must be dominant – the one faced with the problem about which the story revolves.

From these two characters the necessary conflict stems, whatever its quality – emotional, competitive, or even based on a form of vendetta, though this would need an upbeat ending to avoid any hint of bitterness.

Short story readers don't want to be depressed. They read short stories because they can do so in moments snatched out of a busy day; also because they enjoy them and want to continue to, so the main character is usually presented sympathetically. Remember that his or her role is to overcome the main problem. How this is achieved is the basis of the whole plot, though character number two will also be essential to it.

In a romantic short story, conflict could arise through thwarted love, rejection, jealousy, infidelity, a rift between lovers, or non-marital problems between sexual partners – and never forget that whatever your personal views, they have no place in your story. If you want to write contemporary fiction, you must be aware of, and accept, contemporary behaviour and outlook.

Time and space

In the short story there is no room for overcrowding with too many characters, slabs of lengthy narrative, prolonged reminiscence or retrospection. Flashbacks must be fleeting, and only used if there is no other way to throw light on an issue.

One effective way to do this is through a flash of memory in the leading character's mind; the recollection or reminder of an incident or scene which stirred the current conflict. Such a recollection can get the story on its way or take it a big step forward at a crucial moment, but *never at any time must it be allowed to put a brake on the action.*

In this respect dialogue is more useful than many aspiring authors realise. Two voices in discussion can reveal two sides of a question in far less time than it takes to explain it from only one person's viewpoint. It also avoids unnecessary wordage and holds or increases a reader's interest.

Over-writing will kill a short story from the start, but this doesn't mean that brevity must reduce it to the level of a synopsis. Conflict and action must be as well sustained in a short story as in a novel, but in the short story the art lies in making every word count in a compact space.

This skill does not come easily. It comes through perseverence and a serious analysis of published short stories – not a casual read here and there, but a regular in-depth study of construction and treatment. Enquire at your local library for books of short stories most frequently borrowed and, if your aim is for the magazine market, study those in which you want to be published. Do so for a period of at least four months, analysing not only the fiction, but the features and advertisements and the regular 'interests' pages. From these you can learn a lot.

If, for instance, advertisements regularly include stair-lifts and necessary comforts for the aging, and the letters pages include letters from proud grannies and/or proud mums, and the cookery pages feature dishes for four to six servings, and home pages include regular advice on home ownership, and fiction includes stories based on parental versus teenage problems, domestic dramas and the like, then you have an obvious market for stories about family life.

Magazine covers also indicate the age for which they cater, from teenager to the turned-thirties to the mature forties and on. Fashion and beauty pages do the same. All are clear sign-posts, and all need close study to supplement *regular* analysis of the editorial and fiction pages. Unless an author sustains this market study, the frequent changes in editorial policy (which happen when sales fluctuate and public tastes change) will be missed – and so will the author's targets.

The right attitude and the right approach

Many non-writers imagine that the short story is easy to write; that it is only a question of tossing off a few hundred words in spare moments. This indicates a lack of appreciation of a literary form which is an art in itself, and this ignorance is often demonstrated by such remarks as, 'I read a story of yours in a woman's mag when I was under the dryer today. Of course, I don't read that sort of thing normally, but at the hairdresser's there's nothing better to do . . .', or, 'My dear, *I* could write the stuff you write if only I had the time.'

Patronage hurts as much as adverse criticism. Both can undermine a writer's confidence, but the wise one learns that hurt pride can become a handy weapon. After such encounters let it whip your imagination into action.

Take either of the stupid remarks quoted above and you have the basic ingredient for a short story about a woman with a tactless tongue (a universal characteristic of gossips), and since they exist at all social levels the traditional village gossip is the first to spring to mind. In addition, the restricted background of a village can be helpful in the limited space of a short story. Bear in mind that a short story must be precisely that – a *short* story – which brings me to the necessary restriction in the number of characters.

Assembling your cast

Two main characters can sometimes need the support of a third or even a fourth, but only if essential to the plot, and often so briefly that their entrances can be almost transient. They may not even appear on the scene. They can be introduced through one of the main character's thoughts, such as a mother wondering how a big step she is contemplating will be received by her teenage daughter. The reader sees the girl through the mother's mind; she is brought to life in a few words and then not re-introduced, but her influence over her mother's decision can be the climax of the tale.

Like a change of scene when a story stumbles and threatens to die, the injection of a subsidiary character can bring a flagging story to life; so when you sense disaster, look at your cast combined with your plot in the way a dramatist does when his curtain threatens to descend prematurely.

Another reason may be that your plot isn't strong enough to stand on its own and that an infusion of new blood might revive it. My own practice at such a point is to examine my main character to find if the weakness lies there. If not, then I look at the main supporting character.

The need for supplementary help always makes itself felt; examining and heeding it can bring new life to a flagging story.

Speed and tempo

To speed up action, some characters can be useful without being seen. Letters and 'phone calls can be useful substitutes. Both can bring news that marks a turning point in the story or even heralds the climax, but this manouevre can only be acceptable if the caller or letter-writer has already been referred to by name so that the reader is already aware of them, like secondary characters waiting in the wings.

Never must totally new characters be produced like rabbits out of a hat at the climax of a story, or credulity will be destroyed. The reader will feel defrauded, and so will any editor who reads and, not surprisingly, rejects it. Equally, 'cheat' endings (such as the *'it was all a dream!'* ploy which heads all editors' black lists) will guarantee rejection.

If it is vital for a subsidiary character to play a part, it must be brief but effective. The main character, their problem and the way they deal with it, must be the pivotal point from start to finish.

A good exercise is to analyse a simple love story, usually written from the woman's angle. You will find that she takes centre stage throughout and that everything is seen and felt through *her* heart and *her* mind, whether written in first or third person, past or present tense.

In contrast, many a successful short story has been told through the eyes of a close bystander, such as (to conjure up an imaginary situation) a grandparent who is concerned about a problematic twelve-year-old grandson. From his side of the wide age gap, detachment enables the old man to see the cause of the trouble – self-absorbed parents who over-indulge the boy to keep him out of their way and cannot understand why he 'should turn out like this when they have always given him everything he wanted'.

There is a choice here.

(1) To make the old man the main character, telling the story through his eyes so the problem becomes his – whether to interfere and take the parents to task, even threatening to seek custody of the boy.
(2) To make the boy the main character, telling the story through his unhappy young mind. That would be a supreme test of a writer's skill, for an unhappy child has many problems and all bewildering, and not everyone has a sound knowledge of child psychology.
(3) To focus on one or other of the parents, possibly the mother since mothers (at least, the majority) are forever conscious of the tie of motherhood and easily caught in an emotional tug-of-war.

A fourth approach could be through the joint parents, bewildered because their child, once so amenable, has become so hard to handle. As each blames the other, so more conflict arises.

Of the three main angles the first, for me, holds the stronger appeal because I see the grandfather as a man whose age and experience has made him wise and compassionate, a man to whom an unhappy, mixed-up boy might respond.

Why not give your imagination an airing by pursuing one, or all, of these options?

Developing the tale

Let's go back to the village gossip. Since gossips exist everywhere, though traditionally in an enclosed community, the background could just as easily be an office where staff rivalry exists, or a local tennis club or dramatic society or golf club, or a local women's guild or bridge club – even an all-mens' club, for not only women are gossips!

Any of these would adapt well to the limitations of length and number of characters, focusing on the main character who is the gossip's target and secondly on the gossip, but although any of the above settings may seem restrictive, it cannot be taken for granted that a village setting is necessarily so. Since travel and communications have reached their present peak (and beyond, which is fine for sci-fi authors), a sense of a wider world beyond village confines can be achieved by suggestion rather than by lengthy description. This can apply to many settings, such as in one short story I wrote about an air pilot and a stewardess during a flight to Jordan.

At that time the journey from Heathrow to Amman took five and a half hours, so the limitation of time was already set and the physical limitation of space was confined to the aircraft. Even the couple's personal contact was controlled by the closed door of the flight deck and restricted to moments when she took essential refreshments to the air crew. In those moments her tension heightened because they had quarrelled before take-off and her longing to make it up was frustrated by his determination to avoid her eye.

So for five and a half hours the conflict between them flourished silently in an atmosphere which could have been claustrophobic but which was not so because of an awareness of the vast space through which they were flying. This was created by indication rather than by descriptive passages; passing references to the changing light as the plane flew from one hemisphere into another, a glimpse of the staggering Turkish coastline, the relentless approach of Amman airport where the pilot would hand over to another while she, not yet so privileged as to earn a twelve-hour break before turnaround, remained on duty for the return flight. Emotion became taut and remained so to the end – which was *not* brought about by a crash landing or a slice of hospital drama, but by an incident highlighting their stupidity and both having the sense to acknowledge it.

Other vital points

It has been said that the short story 'conforms to one mood, one style, and one pace'.

I disagree with the first point. Good atmospheric writing subtly reflects the prevailing and changing moods and emotions of the main character or characters, so that the reader is drawn into them and gripped until the end.

As for style, this can cover the satirical, the humorous, the sentimental, the serious – whatever treatment you feel is right for the tale you have to tell. You would not, for instance, tell a basically sad story in a satirical or humorous tone. The story itself governs your choice, and with experience a writer knows instinctively the style in which it must be written.

The same applies to tenses – whether the story should be written in the past or present tense, and in first or third person. There is even a fourth – the angle of a looker-on, such as the grandfather of the unhappy twelve-year-old. Let *him* tell the child's story and see how it differs from one told by the child's father, and different again from the mother's.

Finding and harnessing short story ideas

The sources for ideas explored in Chapter 3 can be applied to all types of fiction, but selectivity is particularly necessary where the short story is concerned.

Many a novel has been based on fully documented press reports of public and private people and events; on detailed TV documentaries; on scandals revealed by competitive press sources. All such novels have needed intensive research, checking facts and digging for more, sifting the true from the false or evaluating how much can reasonably be used and how much left to the imagination.

For the short story the *sources* for ideas need not be so extensive as for the novel. For many you need delve no further than an eye-catching headline or magazine blurb. A skim through editorial captions in magazines and newspapers can yield plenty. Letters to the Editor and the Agony Aunt's page are particularly fertile.

Here are a few authentic 'screamers': '*My nightmare – I won't see my little girl for five years.*' '*Women who choose to live alone.*' '*We swapped clothes for the day.*' '*Why we tell our secrets to strangers.*'

Take them one by one. Each presents a pertinent question.

Just *why* wouldn't she see her little girl for five years? In the mind's eye a fraught mother's face leaps into view, watching her child being taken away from her. By whom? A woman in an official uniform? A man carrying a child to the departure sign on a railway station or airport, his back relentless?

Questions and answers come instinctively. Is the uniformed woman a police constable? Is she taking the child into safe custody for the five years her mother is to be jailed? Or is the man her ex-husband, granted custody of his daughter following a bitter divorce – and where is he taking her? Far away to his newly acquired Zimbabwe tea plantation? And will the child become estranged from the mother in such a contrasting environment over such a period of time? And how long will the mother have to fight to get the child back? And has she sufficient money? If not, how will she raise it? *There* is the start of a tale which could serve the short story or novel equally well.

What of the others? '*Women who choose to live alone*' suggests a behind-the-scenes story of life in a nunnery, emotionally tense or tranquilly happy, repressed or fulfilled. In contrast, the headline also suggests a contemporary tale about contemporary women, since there are many who cherish their independence nowadays, both physically and professionally.

As for swapping clothes for a day, many identical twins have done that for a joke, to fool people; and many a short story could arise from the situation, such as two sisters hoodwinking their boyfriends at a local gig. The headline can also suggest transvestisism. For this an author would need to have a psychological understanding of such sexual deviance and targeting the right market would not only need care, but be difficult.

In contrast, confiding secrets to strangers offers great scope. It is not unusual between travellers. People in need of a confidant feel safe because the stranger will go out of his or her life, so there can be no betrayal and no embarrassing future meeting.

Enter the *what if* question again. What if a woman travelling from Brighton to London confides to a sympathetic stranger that she has been weekending with a man whom her husband dislikes? She is now ashamed and fears her husband's reaction should he ever find out that she has not been attending a weekend school reunion, as she had pretended, and is too enamoured to end the affair even so – and what if, at Victoria Station, her husband is waiting for her, greets the stranger with pleasurable surprise and proudly introduces his wife . . . and what if the stranger isn't so trustworthy after all and starts a nasty little game of blackmail?

This brings us to the type of short story most in demand today, world-wide.

The tale with a twist

Because it is short and easy to read, many people imagine it is easy to write – until they try it, or until it is rejected and even the most self-critical examination fails to explain why. The plot

47

seems good and so does the writing; the characters are convincing and so is the dialogue; as for the ending, it is all it should be . . .

Or is it? The ending of a twist story should surprise, shock, or leave readers laughing at their own vulnerability. ('*Why didn't I guess?*')

They didn't guess because they missed carefully concealed hints strategically planted but all, like the story itself, brief. The reason for brevity is that a twist-in-the-tale story must fit into a single page and still allow room for illustration.

Factors governing this brevity can be ever-rising production costs, circulation wars, and the fact that few people have time nowadays to read lengthy instalments of fiction. Most are hard-pressed business executives, women as well as men, or on-the-go commuters with time to scan only the shortest of stories or features of human interest. For this reason the short story of 4000 to 5000 words has yielded to that of 1500 or 1000 words, or even fewer. Some are as short as 500!

This change in the United Kingdom women's magazine market is largely due to the influence of the German magazines, *Best* and *Bella,* brought here by their publishers, H Bauer and Gruner & Jahr, in the 1980s. Their brief stories were right on target for busy women with diminishing time for reading, and they marked the end of the lengthier romantic short stories and serials. Fortunately, magazines like *Woman's Weekly* and *My Weekly* still publish longer stories, but the 'short-short', 'coffee break', and 'tale-on-a-page' story makes a regular appearance in their pages too.

The good side of this fiction revolution is that while there is a restriction on length there is less restriction on theme, so market opportunities for male authors have increased. The 'quicky-tale' adapts well to many categories – Crime, Sci-fi, Humour, Psychic, Adventure and Occult, to name a few – but less to the Historical, which demands a more detailed and wider back-ground and is currently more appreciated on the small screen by a visually-orientated audience.

Rules for the tale-twister

These are few, but vital. Length restriction means that characters must come over visually with little or no description; a casual but vivid touch is sufficient to indicate their looks. Mainly they must be 'seen' through their behaviour, their thoughts, their actions, their reactions, and their emotions. Dialogue is the best way to convey them all. And the central character should be focused immediately, preferably in the first line.

Most important is the surprise element. Readers want to be surprised, indeed they expect to be, and are disappointed if they are not, so surprise must be the climax. Readers feel let down if it doesn't come; even more if they guess a dénouement. So beware of the contrived ending which fools no one.

How to get that twist in the tale?

My own way is that of many others – get the ending first and then 'think backward'.

This is rather like walking away from the target but keeping your eye on it whilst travelling back to the beginning, all the time asking *what if?* again. In that way one can sometimes get a double twist – '*What if the first target twists again?*'

A double twist is a double winner; a triple twist is even more so but the most difficult to write. If your ambition extends that far, study the short stories of Scott Fitzerald. As well as being a foremost novelist of the twenties, he was also the finest exponent of the double and triple twist story. With practice an author can master both, but the beginner would be wise to concentrate on the single twist.

It doesn't have to be breathtaking or dramatic, but it *must* be unexpected. Since example is a good form of demonstration, the following two 'twisters' which I wrote for *Woman's Realm* serve as illustration.

The Love Letter

'It's the shock of finding such a letter,' I say to Monica, trying to keep a tremor from my voice and failing. 'It's knocked me for six.'

'I can imagine,' she answers in her calm way. Nothing ever fazes Monica. Poise is one of the assets that make her the permanent leading lady of our local drama group, together with her looks and a talent for acting which I lack. That's why I'm general dogsbody to the group; any chore that needs attention. Sometimes I watch from the prompt corner, wishing for even a tiny part, but the most I get is walk-ons and noises-off.

'Where on earth did you find it?' she asks.

'In his blazer pocket.'

'Surely you don't go snooping in his pockets! I didn't do that with Hugh, even when I had good reason. It's as bad as a husband ferreting through his wife's handbag!'

'Isn't *this* good reason?' I hold out the letter, begging her to read it. But she resists, which surprises me. Monica has been my confidante for years, always ready with advice and help – like when Pete Saunders jilted me at seventeen and I thought it was the end of the world.

'Forget him,' she'd said. 'He's a twit. George Henderson is worth a dozen of him. Open your eyes and take a look.'

So I opened them and I looked and became Bridget Henderson when I was twenty.

'I was *not* snooping!' I protest now. 'This morning he asked me to take his blazer to the cleaners, so I emptied the pockets.'

I'm still holding out the letter. Monica's perfectly manicured hand takes it reluctantly. Even at this hour of the morning, in her designer jeans and matching £200-plus denim jacket, she looks as if she's stepped straight off the catwalk. Her shining brown hair is coiled in a French pleat; her make-up just right. I am suddenly aware of my tangled copper locks. This morning allowed no more than a flick of a comb before the breakfast rush and getting Emma off to school; then I'd put Timmy in his buggy and wheeled him here, driven by my need to see Monica.

Timmy's asleep beside me on a sofa upholstered in Italian brocade and I'm conscious of my ancient corduroys and crumpled T-shirt, stained by splodges of porridge aimed unerringly across the breakfast table. A future darts champ, our Timmy.

Monica grimaces at the writing paper. Cheap. Purple. *Scented*. It offends her taste.

'Says a lot about the woman who chose it, doesn't it? But wait until you read what she says!' The quiver is back in my voice.

I wait as she scans it. When she reaches the reference to nights of passion at Sonning I say, 'That must have been when George was redecorating The Riverside Inn and stayed during the week.'

'There's no address.'

'Less incriminating, leaving it off, I suppose.'

'Was there no postmark, either?'

'No envelope. He must have thrown it away. I don't know any 'Dot', do you?'

Absently, she shakes her head. She's deep in thought. I wait. Then she rouses. 'It could be someone living in Sonning or someone he meets there.' Again, she scans the purple prose. 'My poor Bridget.'

'I've come to you because all the advice you've ever given me has proved right and you've been a good friend to both of us.'

I glance at George's handiwork – peach walls, white paintwork, china niches edged in gold. Monica employed him to redecorate the whole place when he started on his own after redundancy. Her roving husband's alimony is enough for her to maintain the style she'd enjoyed during their brief marriage.

She hands the letter back to me, holding it like something the cat's brought in.

'What can I do?' I plead.

'Well, darling, one thing I would *not* do, is put up with it.'

'You mean – leave him?'

'Issue an ultimatum. Either her – or you.'

'But what if I lost?'

'Then it would *be* no loss.'

'Oh, but it would! More than I could bear. I love him.'

She looks at me with compassion. 'Dear Bridgy. Life is bloody sometimes.'

'You're right, as always. Even so, I'm getting rid of this.'

A fire burns in the elegant Adam-style grate. I throw the letter on the flames. 'You've destroyed the evidence,' she says gently. 'Not that there won't be plenty more from a woman of that sort.'

I nod, unable to speak. I pick up Timmy and carry him out. Monica waits while I fasten him into his buggy outside. As I turn to go, she stops me.

'Surely you wouldn't want a man who meets with a vulgar woman like that? It's insulting.'

'I know you're right, but . . .'

'You'll issue that ultimatum?'

'I'll think about it. All's fair in love, I suppose.'

I look back, smile and wave. She waves too, unsmiling.

To my surprise, George comes home with Emma. 'I finished early, so picked her up at school. Ask if your mother will babysit this evening.'

'Bother, the drama group is auditioning – I was hoping for a part this time.'

He smiles. 'Skip it, darling. We've something to celebrate. I've won that contract I tendered for! Now I can delegate to my new man.'

'You mean Watkins, the handsome one?'

'If you like the type. Apparently Monica does. She rang to say that *he* should finish the work at her place. Can't think why, but I'm glad. Keeping her at bay is a strain . . .'

I hide a smile. How wise it had been to show her that letter! A woman so fastidious could never tolerate such a vulgar rival.

Right then, Emma bursts in, clutching something. 'Mum! May I have this writing pad for drawing on? Its a lovely purple. And it's *scented*, too!'

A Taste of Freedom

Well, I've done it. I've left him. I've finally said goodbye and walked away, but the reproach in his eyes goes with me, filling me with guilt.

I didn't expect to feel this way. I've known this separation was inevitable. I've even looked forward to it, relishing the thought of the freedom, the space in which to be myself – just like my friend Helen. We went to school together, grew up together, bridesmaided for each other, exchanged confidences . . .

'You'll be thankful, Jenny. What you must do now is make the most of your freedom. God knows, you've earned it. Come to my aerobics class – it'll do you good, take you out of yourself. You've always been too much of the home slave.'

'Don't I have to enrol, or something?'

'The class isn't full yet. Meet me there and I'll get you in.'

'But I haven't anything to wear. Don't I need one of those Lycra outfits?'

'You can buy them at the leisure centre shop. Leotard and tights to match, all in gorgeous colours. Come on, Jenny. You'll love it. Makes you feel great and really knocks off the inches.'

That I could certainly do with, but right now I need to drive away the memory of that expression in his eyes and the awful feeling of guilt – ridiculous, of course, because I've nothing in the world to feel guilty about.

When I reach the leisure centre Helen takes one look at me and says, 'My goodness, you look as if you've shot someone! Snap out of it, darling. You're here to enjoy yourself.'

Surprisingly, I do, although I don't realise it until afterwards, when exercise and rhythm have set my blood flowing.

The glamourous Lycra outfit is gorgeous and so easy to move in that I feel no guilt about the price – only about what I've done to him. Every beat of the music reminds me. . .

'*Step – step – step – step – STEP – step – step . . .*'
'*How – can – you – do– THIS – to – me . . . ?*'

and there he is, looking straight at me with the dark eyes I love so much, asking his silent question. *How can you do this to me?*

Oh, damn the music, drumming the words into my brain, words he didn't utter, a question I saw only in his eyes.

Suddenly the brief exhilaration is gone and guilt is dominant again. Were women born feeling guilty, I wonder. And do all women feel this way in situations like this?

I drop out of the class, flop on a seat by the wall and close my eyes, which is just about the worst thing I can do because there he is again and I feel more than guilt now; I feel a longing to get away from here, to go back, to reassure him, to let him know that I'd never abandon him.

'Are you all right, Jenny?' Helen asks. 'It's a bit strenuous the first time, I know. Anyway, we have a break now, then another half-hour's session, and after that we can toddle off to the Marquis of Granby for a drink. Low alcohol, of course.' She laughs. Then she does a double-take. 'My dear, surely you're not going? Surely you enjoyed – '

'Yes, yes, I did!' I fling the words over my shoulder while heading for the changing room. There's plenty of time, I know, but I can't wait.

I change in record time, take the lift down to the car park, and before long I'm racing in top gear. When I see rain on the windscreen, I switch on the wipers mechanically, but the glass doesn't clear . . . it's me . . . eyes brimming. I'm thinking of all the good times . . . of the way he enjoys life, but isn't enjoying it now . . . of the fun, even the squalls, and I want it all back. I want everything to go on as before. I don't want empty days. If this is freedom, anyone can have it. All right, Helen love, I'm a home slave. You can think that if you want to. I like what I am, what I was, and what I'm going to keep right on *being* – but don't worry, I'll keep on with the aerobics . . .'

By the time I reach my destination I am admirably self-controlled. At least, I think I am. I adjust the car mirror and touch up my hair and my face, calming myself. It won't do to let him see I'm upset.

And suddenly he's there – but not alone. He's in the middle of a group and he's laughing. Laughing!

Then he sees me and comes running, carrying something with care.

'Look! ' he cries. 'Look what *I* made on my first day at school!'

Analysis

The art of the twist story lies in the subtle placing of red herrings. In *A Taste of Freedom* the first appears in the opening words, 'Well, I've done it. I've left him. I've finally said goodbye . . .', suggesting that she has left her husband or partner after much thought. This is confirmed in the second paragraph with, 'I've known this separation was inevitable . . .' and in the third with her friend's assurance that she has 'always been too much of a home slave' and has earned her freedom.

The red herring then dangles throughout the story, emphasized by her increasing sense of guilt – 'Do all women feel this way in a situation like this?' – so the reader continues to believe it is one kind of situation only.

But clues have been scattered. First with her defensive reflection that she really has nothing to feel guilty about, confirmed by her matter-of-fact friend, then with her anxiety 'to reassure him that I'd never abandon him' and, later, by her longing for everything to go on as before – ' . . . the fun, even the squalls . . .'. Today the word 'abandon' is predominantly associated with deserted children. Had her anxiety been for her husband, it would have been more natural to want to assure him that she would never leave him, 'leave' being a more adult word associated with the end of a partnership.

The second clue was again a misleading word. Adults have quarrels, even rows, but with children there are squalls, and even these can be missed when children go to school and the house takes on an unnatural silence.

All this enabled me to place the twist in its rightful place – the final line.

How did the idea come? By the method suggested earlier, recalling a moment from long ago – delivering my son for his first day at school and feeling as if I had thrown him to the wolves.

In contrast to *A Taste of Freedom, The Love Letter* scattered no clues. It depended entirely on the wife's emotional appeal to a long-standing friend and although the reader was intended to mistrust the elegant Monica and to sympathise with the wife's decision to show her an incriminating letter from a distasteful rival, the truth incriminated no one until the final line.

Examination of both stories reveals that they have something in common – both are based on ordinary domestic situations, emotionally driven and therefore lending themselves well to first person writing. Exploration of domestic relationships offers great material for any sphere of fiction writing and, in the case of the short story, manifold incidents to draw upon.

5. Characterization

Bringing characters to life

Unless a character springs to life as vividly as a charismatic actor onstage, my own practice is to let them lie fallow in my mind. In this way they become familiar to me. The longer I live with them the more real they usually become, but occasionally they can prove to be stubborn. When that happens, and if they insist on remaining static, I discard them because they are obviously not going to develop in any helpful way, nor will they prove to be malleable should I attempt to reshape them. Such characters then have to be replaced by others and the whole procedure starts again. That is part of the job and worth the perseverence.

Building character portraits

In the previous chapter I indicated how the hapless theatrical dresser in *The Mating Dance* came to mind after much fruitless searching. The interesting thing was that the unfeeling leading lady presented herself without any searching at all. I sometimes find that when one character occurs to me another, in complete contrast, follows as a necessary foil. If not, I have to look for one.

This can happen if I stub my toes on a casting problem, such as having too many laudable characters or too many less laudable. An even balance is desirable because it is the characters who give light and shade to a story. Without contrast in looks and personalities, in manners and morals, in behaviour and intelligence, in upbringing and background, a storyteller's pictures will be painted in dull monochrome.

Good characterization emerges from the interplay of differing temperaments. Contrasting characters are therefore not only valuable, but essential. Their very differences set up chain reactions and spur the story forward, so it is wise to bear in mind that every character, be it in a novel or short story, must react individually to any situations in which they are involved.

It is therefore advisable for an inexperienced writer to know every possible detail about them before starting to write. If characters don't progress beyond the dummy stage in a writer's mind, they won't get very far, and nor will the story.

Although it is true that I never draw up a long and detailed synopsis of the story (I like to surprise myself as much as my readers – it keeps my interest alive), I do make notes as characters and situations occur to me even though, when I begin the actual writing and action develops, both are likely to change as an inevitable result of their differing personalities.

New writers, however, will find character dossiers helpful, not only when it comes to character portrayal but by sparking situations which will arise *because* of their differing natures. Detailed pen portraits will register their individual traits, their looks, their idiosyncracies, their backgrounds, their likes and dislikes, their attitudes, their beliefs, and every detail which might otherwise be forgotten or overlooked. The mere act of recording them will be a spur to your pen and increase your awareness of them – but don't be surprised if subsidiary characters present themselves along the way, thrusting themselves in as the story develops.

This usually happens when you are well launched and is a sure sign that your imagination is working well and that you are thinking creatively. They arrive for a purpose, to contribute to the action, so make the most of them. Take good stock of them, analyse them, and record notes about them so that when they re-enter, even after a long lapse of time, they will need no re-creation or reintroduction because you will have all their characteristics at your fingertips, making them instantly recognisable.

Personal involvement

The most enjoyable part of fiction writing, to me, is becoming involved with a novel as it unfolds, so that I am not only part-creator but part-participator. I am *in* there with my characters and when they 'take over' they carry me with them. When this happens to you, discard any idea that you must force them back onto pre-set tracks. Try that and the exciting, personal contact will be lost and that will show itself in the story.

At no time must you allow yourself to become a mere puppet-master, jerking the strings. You must bring your characters to life and, at the risk of repetition, I stress again that to do that you must live with them before you even start writing your story. Get to know them and you will find that their behaviour will come naturally and with little or no prompting from you. Remember what Coleridge said when reviewing *The Mysteries of Udolpho* – 'In the search for what is new, an author is apt to forget what is natural.' In other words, forcing your characters into unnatural behaviour because you are seeking new and exciting ways in which to make them perform, can spell disaster.

How can I best describe the way in which characters 'take over'? It is something that *happens* and you will recognise it and welcome it when it does. Some authors call it 'getting lost in the story', and that seems a fair way of describing it, although the onus of responsibility will still be on you, their creator. You must know your cast so intimately that when one of them starts to behave 'out of character', you are aware of it. When such a situation arises you must overcome it by searching for the reason.

Sometimes a scene can suddenly stumble and, try as you may, you cannot rescue it. Invariably, the blame lies not with some-*thing* but with some*one*. You have unconsciously allowed a character or characters to behave unnaturally, or have tried to push them in the wrong direction.

This is where your pen portraits come to the rescue. Take out your dossiers, study them carefully and, almost unfailingly, you will realise where, and with whom, the fault lies. You must then go back, scrap the faulty scene and, after reassessment and much thought, re-write from the point at which things began to go wrong. In that way you will get back on the right track and the action will proceed.

Or you may find that the scene fell down at the point where a supplementary character should have been introduced. The arrival of a new face can often help to turn an awkward corner, *provided that it has a useful part to play, however briefly*. Never forget that even small-part characters, like small-part players onstage, must be as real and convincing as your leads because their minor contributions are just as essential to the story's development.

Actions and reactions

Always remember that the actions and reactions of every person in your story, however important or unimportant, must not only stem from the kind of person they are but also, as the story progresses, the kind they become. People change in real life as a result of their experiences. They must do the same in fiction or 'believability' will die and so will a reader's urge to read on. It therefore stands to reason that an author should know a great deal more about the characters in his story than is ever revealed to the reader except by implication.

The cliché that 'actions speak louder than words' is as true as it ever was, but how can an author reveal a character's actions without knowing him or her in depth? In this respect, nothing can be more helpful than individual dossiers, word portraits with which to refresh your memory when needful.

Before you start building up your portrait gallery, a word of warning – avoid modelling fictional characters on living people, or on people you know; don't even model them on people with whom you are merely acquainted. Therein can lie danger. Some people are all too eager to identify with fictional characters, especially if they are acquainted with the author and on the lookout for evidence that they 'have been used'.

Despite assertions that people never recognise themselves because their personal idea of what they are like is the reverse of reality, it is not unknown for readers to make claims to the contrary. Such claims have sometimes resulted in libel actions, unpleasant to encounter even when dismissed from the courts.

'I'm afraid of talking to you in case you put me in one of your novels!' The remark was once made to me, somewhat archly, by a woman I scarcely knew. Her fears (or hopes?) were groundless. I find it impossible to base my characters wholly on people I know or meet. Mannerisms may register and even creep in unconsciously, but never real characters as a whole because we are acquainted only with the personalities they present to the world. This is supported by Graham Greene's admission that he could never model a complex fictional character on a real-life acquaintance, because he needed to know much more about the innermost thoughts and feelings of a character than he could ever learn about any living person, no matter how close to him the living person might be.

Nothing could be more true. Consciously or unconsciously, we all hide certain truths about ourselves – even *from* ourselves – because the inner core of every human being is solitary and remains so throughout life. Perhaps that is why people crave emotional security, to *belong,* to love and be loved. You will find, the longer you write, that love in all its varied manifestations, by no means only sexual, is one of the strongest character motivations of all. From it stem countless emotional situations.

Another danger in modelling your fictional characters on real life acquaintances, taking characteristics from here and others from there, is that you will produce very sketchy portraits instead of flesh and blood, 'warts 'n'all' human beings. Fictional characters need to be portrayed in depth. This is the object of assembling three-dimensional pictures of your characters. You will be establishing them firmly in your mind from the embryo stage, so start your individual dossiers as each character takes hold of your imagination, even those who are only hazy and who may well remain so; the ineffectual ones whom you may eventually discard. Their presence in your portrait gallery will serve to spotlight the importance of others on whom you will then focus more attention. It is these who will become your cast, ready to step onstage.

Always remember that any character who does not actively advance the story is unnecessary to it. Their presence in your portrait gallery will single them out because they will be diminished by others on whom you will instinctively focus.

I suggest you prepare each character dossier along the following lines.

The importance of age

Make particular note of birth dates so that when writing, you can maintain consistency. This is particularly important when writing a story spanning a number of years, when it is essential that a characer should remain at the right age throughout and not be, for instance, twenty-one at the start and thirty-one only five years later.

Noting birth dates will also help you to visualise their growth from childhood and through the progression of time. Even though you may not write of them retrospectively, or refer much to their childhood or youth, you will have a greater depth of feeling for them if you know exactly when they were born and what life was like throughout their formative years, all of which has inevitably left its mark.

Age is also important when depicting behaviour. In this it plays as vital a part as physical growth or physical deterioration.

(Notice how the voices of elderly people can become gruffer or more highly pitched, or quavering and breathless). Remember too that age can influence a person's attitudes, not only to younger people but to life and morals and politics and religion, and that in the young, particularly in teenagers, age can demonstrate itself in boisterous behaviour or shyness, impudence or sulkiness, *gaucherie* or bravado, defiance or brash self-confidence. In the very young it can reveal a touching dependence on, or trust in, their elders or, in disturbed children, sometimes a fear of them.

Watch children on their way to school; do they go willingly or with dragging feet? Do they run along with others, or walk alone? Watch them, too, in shops or buses. Studying them when out with their parents can be very revealing. How often do you see an obviously united family? How often does the father tag along while the mother is absorbed in the children? Or how often does a child walk forlornly while the parents are absorbed in each other?

Degrees of intimacy in personal relationships can be detected even in the most commonplace situations. Watch out for them and you will be nearer to understanding human nature. Then add the results of your observations to the 'Age' section of your dossier.

Bear in mind that social behaviour and social etiquette throughout the centuries has varied considerably; therefore in a realistic historical novel the attitude of younger people toward older ones, of men toward women and women toward men, must be vastly different from today, whatever the period. As an example, in Victorian times the manners of well brought up youths toward their elders would be obedient and respectful, no matter what feelings or thoughts smouldered beneath. In a modern story the reverse can be true and personal opinions and attitudes freely expressed – and what scenes and verbal exchanges can arise from them!

Parent/child relationships vary from generation to generation, and to depict such changes realistically it is necessary to study the background and level of society against which you are setting your story. Authenticity is vital; without it, conviction will be lacking. This is where research comes in, a subject I discuss more fully in Chapter 11.

Another thing to strive for, when you are depicting age in relation to behaviour and dialogue, is that it should be typical of the character. Don't, for instance, make him or her behave like a person twenty years younger unless the character itself, such as a woman clinging to her youth, affects such behaviour and mannerisms. If she does, demonstrate them whenever she makes an entrance, but don't overdo them or she will become a bore. A woman forever striving to be young is likely to be a bore anyway, so make the doses minimal. Light touches can convey more than heavy-handed emphasis.

Bear in mind constantly that whatever a person's age, and despite changes due to physical and mental maturity, fundamental characteristics usually remain unchanged. Think of people you have known for a long time; try to recall them when younger and compare this with the way they are now. They may appear to have changed beyond recognition, but how often, after talking with them, do you think (sometimes with amusement) that he or she 'hasn't changed a bit', they are still blunt and proud of it, or still shy, or still garrulous, or still just that little bit vain?

It will also be useful to realise that, in one particular way, age never changes a person – and that is in their capacity to be hurt. They may hide it more easily, but the belief that 'the torments of youth' cease as people grow older is far from the truth. Emotions don't become shallower. They become deeper. In preparing a character dossier for an older person, it is wise to remember that.

Physical attributes

Keep your characters' looks in mind by recording such details as colouring, facial features, blemishes (such as moles and birthmarks), height, weight and other individual characteristics. Nothing can be too detailed under this heading, for each item will enhance your visual picture. Note skin texture and tone; hair colour and quality. Note whether a character, particularly female, is likely to ring changes in hairstyles. Note deportment and carriage, speech rhythms, pet slang words, accent or dialect if any, and whether they speak grammatically or ungrammatically. You will then be so familiar with them that they will become as alive to the reader as to yourself.

Voice tones betray a great deal, and so do gestures and mannerisms. 'Body language' can reveal hyperactivity, agitation, laziness, nervousness, self-assurance, confidence, aggressiveness, shyness, and many other traits – but be aware that body language can also be misinterpreted by the inexpert. Poor posture may not be due to awkwardness or clumsiness, but to poor health or physical disability, or even to a lack of confidence resulting from parental criticism or unfavourable comparison with more graceful siblings.

Sitting with eyes downcast, arms tight against the body, glancing quickly at someone and away again, biting worriedly at the lower lip; all can indicate emotional insecurity.

Watch people and make a mental note of such betrayals. Extroverts meet the world frank-eyed and welcoming; introverts invariably do not, but nor do shy people who may well come out of their shells when smiled upon. You will be able to add much useful material to your physical and mental inventory the more keenly you observe your fellow men.

Upbringing and environment

Both these factors have a major effect on the formation of character, therefore the more detailed your knowledge of them, the stronger will be your awareness of them and the more vividly will you present them. Store every detail; whether they were brought up in the city or the countryside, in poor homes, rich homes, comfortable middle-class homes, happy or unhappy homes – and what effect it had on them.

What were their parents like? Was *their* marriage a warm and united one, or did it break up, with an adverse effect on family life? How many brothers and sisters were there, and were they affectionate or quarrelsome – and why? What sort of an education did your characters have, particularly your main one? Did he or she rebel against schooling, or grow up with an unrequited thirst for knowledge? If so, why, in both cases? What of childhood dreams and traumas – what caused them? And what about childhood successes and failures, both of which can have a lifetime's effect and be responsible for future happiness or unhappiness? I can still recall the bitter disappointment of winning an art scholarship when young, and being unable to take it up due to my family's removal to a distant part of the country – and my rebellious teenage behaviour for a long time afterward. Such are only some of the environmental influences from which your characters will grow, finally emerging as complete people in your mind.

But apart from being familiar with a leading character's upbringing and background, a similar knowledge regarding friends and relatives is desirable, even if they never actively enter the story. They will be alive in your main character's mind, and through his or her mind you will come to know them, so concentrate on those who played an important part in their developing years. To focus on one in particular, as Emlyn Williams did in *The Corn is Green* or as Muriel Spark did in *The Prime of Miss Jean Brodie*, can be tremendously productive. From such characters a whole story can grow, authentic in detail and background, richly alive.

Marital status, or lack of it, is always important. On it can hinge the development of many emotional scenes. Similarly, career history and resultant ambitions can play vital parts.

If you think deeply about every aspect of your main characters' backgrounds, and almost as much about the supporting ones, they will become as real to you as your own. You are unlikely to incorporate all such details in your script – to do so would overburden the story – but their influence will be powerful. This is their value to you. They are the colours you will use to paint a more vivid picture, bringing your story strongly to life.

Religious influences

Religion may not play a part in your tale, but you should still take into account its possible effect on a character's personality. A religious background, or lack of it, can colour their development. The influence of a devout family could prevail into adulthood, or wane and then reassert itself in later years, whereas the influence of a bigotted or fanatically religious upbringing has been known to drive a person toward atheism. The influence of religion is revealed in Graham Greene's works and, combined with religious conflict, is the powerful theme in Susan Howatch's *Glittering Images* and its sequels.

Sexuality

It is essential to know the degree of your main character's sexuality, because its influence on character development is important. It is a vital underlying instinct which has a profound effect on personality and behaviour, and therefore on characters and action within the plot. Sexuality does more than arouse physical desires and responses; it influences attitudes to, and assessment of, other people. It stirs the first interested glance, the unspoken question, the calculated approach, the '*Will* she?' and the 'I *hope* he . . .' but, more than that, it can arouse jealousy and despair and feelings as bitter as hatred.

Never has there been so radical a change in fictional requirements as now, particularly in the romantic genre. The physical and moral perfection attributed to the hero prior to World War Two, in women's fiction particularly, along with the 'thoroughly-bad-cad' as his opposite number, were as untrue to life as the beautiful and saintly heroine who never failed to get the handsome hero, and the badder-than-bad-bitch who always got her come-uppence. After the war the market for boy-meets-girl-but-stop-at-the-bedroom-door type of fiction rapidly died. The anti-hero was born and the ordinary heroine, with realistic imperfections, made her entry.

Now another extreme has been reached. Even the sugary-sweet romances of Mills & Boon have undergone radical changes since their link-up with the Canadian publishers, Harlequin. Now the major part of their fiction includes varying levels of sexual explicitness, some of which could fairly be classed as erotica, but in one respect they remain loyal to the past – writers of historical romances still have a market with them.

Since tides have been turning since the world began, it seems reasonable to expect them to continue to – but who knows? The best way for an author to keep an eye on trends in fiction is to study the book pages in newspapers and magazines and the ever-changing titles on bookstands. A good investment is a subscription to *The Bookseller*. If too costly, visit your local library and ask if you may see their copy. Invariably, you will be allowed to read it, but only on the premises.

6. Motivation

Making your characters tick

When a story is rejected as 'implausible' it is immediately assumed that this refers to the plot, whereas the implausibility is more likely to be in character motivation, rendering the whole thing unconvincing.

The reason why the bizarre plots of successful fantasy and horror writers are so popular is because the authors motivate their characters *believably*, making the novels plausible and therefore acceptable. It matters little to their readers that in real life such stories could not be true although, as with well written science fiction, it is always wondered whether they just *might* be, but true devotees of fantasy and horror accept the plots without question, enjoying the thrills and chills.

But would they, if writing and characterization were weak? In the case of Dean Koontz the prose is literary, in Stephen King's it holds a style of its own, and in both cases the plots grip because the motivation of their characters is believable.

Put the plots of Ira Levin's *The Stepford Wives* and *Rosemary's Baby* under the microscope (and even *The Boys from Brazil* although cloning is now accepted as a possibility) and both will appear to be bizarre and unbelievable, but their success is the result of convincing character motivation.

This essential applies to the whole spectrum of popular fiction, whatever the genre. The motivation behind your characters' behaviour will make them either convincing or unconvincing and your book acceptable or unacceptable.

Differing motivations

What are the strongest, and the most common, motivations?

First: **Love.** Too many people give a faint curl of the lip if you admit to writing romance, yet love is a universal and vital

66

emotion. Throughout the ages authors and dramatists and poets have written about love more than they have written about any other human emotion. Shakespeare used it as a powerful motivation in *Romeo and Juliet,* and included it in nearly all his plays, from *Twelfth Night, A Midsummer Night's Dream, The Taming of the Shrew* and *Antony and Cleopatra* to *King Lear,* where the emphasis was on filial devotion. Dickens included it, in all its aspects, in novels which, in his lifetime, were regarded as pulp for the masses but which achieved immortality as classics, even though his characters were larger than life and his prose often flamboyant. His books, because of his skill in characterization and his understanding of motivation, live on.

Love as a motivation is by no means confined to paperback novels like Silhouette Romances. It was vital in Daphne du Maurier's *Rebecca,* an adult Cinderella story elevated to the ranks of accepted literature by stylish writing, excellence of plot, good atmosphere, vivid background, and strongly motivated characters. She also used it with great finesse in her swash-buckling adventure tale, *Frenchman's Creek.* Evelyn Anthony's espionage novels succeed not only because of plot intricacies but because of her deep understanding of, and compassion for, human nature. She uses love movingly and dramatically in books like *The Assassin, The Malaspega Exit, The Tamarind Seed* and, heartrendingly, in *The Rendezvous.* Read any of these books and you will realise the value of love, happy or tragic, as character motivation.

Love has also been, and will forever be, an inspiration to poets and an unending theme for popular songs. Pop stars have grown rich from singing about it and the Brontës, from the depths of their repressed lives, wrote about it with passion. Dumas, Sabatini, George Eliot, Nathaniel Hawthorne, Thomas Hardy and other classical authors introduced it, in all its varied forms, into their works.

Each and every one of us wants to love and be loved. A supportive human relationship is the need of us all. Your readers are the same. Use love as a motivation and you will win their interest, and hold it.

Although love can be one of the most powerful motivations and can be adapted in one form or another to any kind of plot (look at the *crime passionnel*), the dewy-eyed romantic variety can usually serve only the most novelettish of stories. Like all motivations, it needs the support of others to give it strength and impact. **Self-sacrifice** is one – the self-sacrifice of a wife for a husband or a husband for a wife, a mother for her child, a father for his family. There are plenty of permutations on this theme and Dickens used it well in *A Tale of Two Cities*. 'It is a far, far better thing that I do, than I have ever done. . .' said Sydney Carton as he went voluntarily to the guillotine in place of Charles Darnay because he loved the man's wife.

The foregoing demonstrates that one type of motivation alone will not necessarily suffice. Invariably, it needs strengthening with another.

Combining motivations

Below is a list of other motivations which can combine with, or spring from, each other. It is by no means definitive and can be added to with a little thought.

Greed
Jealousy
Revenge
Duty
Fear
Vanity
Hatred
Loneliness

Let's take the first. **Greed** is an unattractive emotion to attribute to a hero, but if he were the anti-hero so popular today, say, a ruthless freedom fighter determined to steal funds to fight a military government's dictatorship and so free the people – it would win a reader's sympathy. Or if he were a hard-up daredevil diving for sunken treasure which, despite the law, he fully intends to keep in order to marry the girl he loves, the reader would be half won over, and completely so were there a well-heeled rival lacking the need or the inclination to risk his neck, and self-satisfied into the bargain. The portrayal of such a rival would thrust sympathy fairly and squarely on to the rogue hero, his greed forgiven. Readers would even be rooting for his success.

Again, the secret of making such a quality acceptable is to combine it with some nobler motive, but it would also be made understandable in a man who has risen from nothing, worked hard at his trade and established his own successful business at long last, only to discover that a life-long friend has swindled him on a vast scale and brought him to bankruptcy.

Revenge would then become the the key motivation; a determination not only to get back every penny, but to get it with added interest and ruin the man in return. Add to this the fact that the life-long friend has also run off with his wife, and you are plunged into the additional motivations of **Hatred** and **Jealousy.** At once you have a more deeply drawn and interesting character, and one very true to life.

By showing readers the *reasons* for a person's behaviour, whether noble or reprehensible, you will paint a more vivid picture. Look at the pen-portrait you have drawn of him, turn to his background details, find the childhood influences or the adverse upbringing which moulded him, and through your greater understanding you will portray him with sympathy, and he will live.

Now, to stimulate your imagination, see what you can do with **Duty, Fear, Vanity** and **Loneliness.** These by no means represent all human motivations, but the vast majority of us are certainly familiar with them; with the possible exception of the first, duty, which was more strongly emphasized in earlier times than it is today, when unquestioning service to king and country, and sometimes to parents and families, has diminished. To associate duty with a period figure may therefore be an easier choice, though to focus on the carers of today (for whom public sympathy is rightly increasing) could be an acceptable angle.

Or take **Loneliness** combined with **Fear.** To me, this immediately suggests a contemporary scene; an old lady too terrified to emerge from her high-rise flat in a violent city area. You could get a scalp-tingling short story out of such a situation if you put yourself thoroughly into the character.

Again, combining **Vanity** with **Fear** immediately conjures up a beautiful but unhappy woman and her fear of aging, of losing her looks, of no longer being admired or wanted; fear that her husband is being unfaithful with someone younger; fear of widowhood and loneliness. This is wonderful material for characterization, bringing so many other motivations into play – resentment, suspicion, bitterness, even slowly corroding hatred of the world and of life.

Think about her and then start writing about her. Your own interpretation will be quite different, bearing your own individual stamp.

As another fillip to your imagination, choose some character known to millions of readers and TV viewers – preferably one who is not a model of virtue, because the 'holier than thou' type warms few hearts, whereas the endearing rake (such as Dickens's Sydney Carton) can seize and hold a reader's interest from the start. A modern example is J R Ewing from the long-running TV 'soap', *Dallas* – still being shown at different times around the world. J R was a reprehensible type who displayed all the flaws any man could possibly be endowed with, yet he stood out in that long-running soap opera as the most memorable figure of all. And while supporting characters are now forgotten, he is not.

J R's believability was not solely due to Larry Hagman's acting, but also to the script writers' thorough motivation of his character. List those motivations for yourself. Draw your own pen-portrait of him. Picture his background, his childhood, his attitudes to others. Plainly, he was jealous of his younger brother, but what made him so? Was he compared unfavourably with him in boyhood? Did girls find Bobby more physically attractive and only want J R when he became head of Ewing Oil? What deep-rooted influences produced his ruthlessness and his callous attitude towards women?

I don't know whether J R's earlier life was ever revealed, but it would seem to have been cushioned against discomfort. Create this earlier life for yourself. What was the influence of his father, or of the ever-patient and homely Ms Ellie? Did he become the school bully and, if so, why? Probe into his past, analyse his character, decide what made him tick and why such a man could win the public's sympathy. You will find endless motivations beneath the complexities of J R's character and then you will know what made it so believable.

But don't use him in any story you propose to sell. He still belongs to the script writers who created him, so any character inspired by him must be wholly new.

Finally, take all the motivations I listed and add to them. Start applying them to your pen-portraits, and your anxiety about bringing characters to life will diminish. You will be creating *live* characters of your own, and you will then be ready to go on to the next important factor – dialogue.

7. Dialogue

Natural v unnatural

It is frequently said that fiction should be the mirror of reality, but this is true only up to a point. Fiction is really the essence of reality distilled into an assimilable form. The same is true of fictional dialogue, which beginners are constantly urged to write as naturally as possible, but if we were to conceal a recorder when two or three people were in 'natural' conversation the result would be a mass of superfluous words, irrelevancies, repetitions, interruptions, contradictions, unfinished sentences and disjointed phrases, all of which, if reproduced for the printed page, would be rambling and pointless, defeating its aim. That aim, as with narrative, should be to advance the story.

The following passage of 'natural' dialogue illustrates what I mean. Two married couples meeting in a coffee shop could sound something like this:

'Hello there, you two! How are you? Oh damn, I forgot to get skin cream from Boots! I'd better go back – no, I'll do it later, I'm *dying* for coffee – no, p'raps I'd better go now or I might forget again. . .'

'Sit down and stop dithering, Mabel. Women!'

'Janet's just the same, old chap. Makes a shopping list and then forgets it. Stinking day, isn't it?'

'Bloody awful.'

'How's the election going down your way?'

'Dunno. Haven't heard.'

'Now don't let's have any politics! Men! It's either that or cricket. Ooh, Jan – I *must* show you the bra I've just bought at that new little French shop!'

'How's the Test Match going, George? Missed it on the telly.'

'This coffee's too strong. Call the girl, Bill.'

'"*She's either too hot or too cold. . . she's either too strong*

71

or too bold. . ." I'll bet that doesn't apply to the pretty one, eh, George? OK, love, I'm calling her.'

'Your husband's very chirpy this morning.'

'Isn't he just! Oh – while I think of it, Mabel – have you *heard* what happened at the Women's Institute? Hilda Turner fairly *spat* because she didn't get on the committee or council or whatever they call it.'

'Thank goodness she didn't! Grace Walker'd be better, look at all the jam she makes. Heavens, you're not going to *wear* that, are you? It's not decent!'

'Well, George likes it. Fetching, he calls it. And I haven't lost my figure yet.'

'Know what I think, Bill? They oughta get Botham back. We'll never win another Test match without him.'

' Gower. That's who they need, old chap.'

'There they go, Jan – cricket again! Well, *I* don't like Grace Walker's jam and she always makes such a *thing* about it, showing off and all that, as if no other woman ever made any. And why d'you call my new bra indecent? Jealous?'

'Listen to 'em. Women!'

'Y'know, I think I *will* go back to Boots. . .'

And so *ad infinitum.*

You can hear conversations like that all too frequently and you could write continuously in that vein without getting any-where or revealing much about the speakers except, in this case, that one wife is scatterbrained, the other a bit of a sour-puss, and both husbands are bores. Such idle chit-chat would hinder rather than advance the action of a story, so let's leave those pedestrian people to their rambling repetitiveness and embark on a scene featuring more useful fictional dialogue.

Let's imagine that a woman is worried about her husband's behaviour. He has become uncommunicative, his manner guarded. On the surface and in the presence of others he is his normal self, but when alone his attitude changes. She feels vaguely threatened by it, particularly since she has recently received menacing 'phone calls in an unrecognisable voice; calls which began shortly after her tycoon father died and she inher-ited his wealth. When telling her husband about the anonymous calls, he had laughed and called her neurotic, but now he is insisting that she needs long term psychiatric help. ('It's well known that women of a certain age can fantasize. You haven't been imagining those 'phone calls again, I hope?') She avoids telling him that, far from imagining them, she is still receiving them and that she suspects the voice to be deliberately muffled, because the more she thinks about it the more she fears that it is his.

What reason could he have?

A good one. She has control of her inherited wealth as long as she is in good health and of sound mind, otherwise that control passes to her husband, and the recession hit his business badly, leaving him heavily in debt.

After weeks of increasing tension, she is desperate to talk to someone. She thinks of her friends, Sylvia and Peter, who live nearby and whom she trusts. Even so, she feels self-conscious when ringing their doorbell, also somewhat guilty because surely no loyal wife would accuse her husband of treachery?

The following approach to the scene would be natural in real life, but overwritten for fiction.

Ruth paused, her finger on the bell push. It was absurd to feel so nervous. After all, they were her personal friends more than they were Ralph's, she and Sylvia having grown up together. She could trust them; they would listen with sympathy and understanding. She found herself insisting on that in her mind.

Sylvia answered the door.

'Ruth, my dear – how lovely to see you! I was saying to Peter only today that I haven't seen you for weeks.' She held the door wide. 'Come along in. How are you? And Ralph, how's he?'

'Fine. Well, we're both fine really.'

Closing the door, Sylvia said, 'What d'you mean – "really"? One of you been a bit off colour? Is that why we haven't seen you at the golf club?'

Ruth followed her into the pleasant living room overlooking the garden. Peter was fiddling with the video. Sylvia said, 'I want him to record the new Inspector Morse – the first since the last series finished, so I don't want to miss it. It's on at nine and we'll be out – Mother's birthday, so of course we must be there.' Peter was absorbed, so his wife tapped him on the shoulder. 'Darling – Ruth's here. How about drinks?'

'Ruth! How nice to see you. Just a tick. . . there, that's it.' Peter rose, kissed Ruth's cheek affectionately and headed for the sideboard.

'What'll you have? The usual?'

'I – I don't think I fancy anything – '

Caught by the bleak note in her voice, Sylvia said in

concern, 'Is something wrong? I thought you looked a bit peaked when I opened the door.'

'Off colour?' asked Peter. 'That's not like you, Ruthie. You're always the picture of blooming health. Here, get this down. It'll do you good.'

But his wife was more perceptive. '*Is* something wrong?'

'As a matter of fact, yes.' Ruth hesitated. 'You'll think I've taken leave of my senses, but – well – I've got to talk to *some*one and you've been my friends for so long. . .'

All too often we linger over preliminaries and exchange pleasantries before getting down to serious conversation, but in fiction such extended dialogue would hold up the action (it could also tempt readers to skip a page or two) so for fiction we must prune it drastically and get to the point.

Like this?

Ruth wasted no time in ringing the doorbell and, to her relief, Sylvia wasted no time in answering it.

'Sylvia!' Ruth gasped. 'You've got to help me! Ralph's trying to have me put away! I'm terrified!'

No, not like that. That's jumping the gun. Let's write it again, bearing in mind that we must convey the essence of the conversation without elaboration.

Ruth was glad when Sylvia promptly opened the door. It gave her no time to hesitate or withdraw.

'Ruth! How nice to see you! Come along in. I was thinking of you only today.' She drew her friend inside, glancing at her in concern. 'Is some thing wrong? You don't look too good.'

'I'm all right – just worried. No. Frightened. I – I thought perhaps I could talk it over with you and Peter, though I expect you'll think I'm imagining things – '

'Now why should we think that?'

'Because it sounds insane to say that Ralph is trying to have me put away.' She reached out, seized her friend's hands and clung to them. 'But that's what I believe. . . !'

Examine those examples while bearing in mind the golden rule that dialogue should advance a story as effectively as a piece of narrative action, and you will recognise that the first passage served no useful purpose because it dawdled amiably before coming to the point; in fact, if you look at it again you will see that it never reached it. The second example also failed because it rushed ahead to make some dramatic impact and resulted in being abrupt and melodramatic, proving that to over-compress dialogue can be as ineffective as overburdening it. The third was acceptable because it distilled the scene down to its essentials, yet retained the emotion. It also cut out Peter's ineffectual contribution (though he could play an effective part later) and clearly indicated Ruth's nervous tension, also her relief because she was given no time to heed her instinct to run away.

Tension was also indicated by her reaching for Sylvia's hands and clinging to them. In addition, her friend's sympathetic character was revealed in her immediate perception of Ruth's anxiety, and finally emotion plus fear were brought to a head when Ruth blurted out the truth. The action was not only ready to move on, but had taken a vital step forward.

How much dialogue to include?

Claims have been made that few novels are bought that contain less than twenty to forty per cent of dialogue, but such claims are confounded by many successful and well written novels, amongst which the Raj novels of Paul Scott spring to mind, as do the crime novels of P D James, whose narrative prose is as alive and telling as her dialogue and enjoyable to read because of its literary quality. It is this literary quality that elevates her books above other crime fiction, but only with time and experience will the average beginner reach such a degree of expertise.

Note that I use the word 'average' because it is certainly not unknown for natural-born writers to produce outstanding first novels; but the vast majority of aspiring authors achieve a high degree of professionalism only through the qualities I named in my opening chapter – dedication, hard work, and enthusiasm. In addition to these essentials they must develop an ear for dialogue.

One good way of doing this is to study not only the works of successful novelists, but of notable playwrights too. Such plays can be obtained from local libraries and good bookshops.

Reading stage dialogue can be not only enjoyable, but instructive. Start with plays like Ira Levin's *Death Trap* and you will see how every spoken line advances the action, reveals character, and helps to create tension and atmosphere. In fiction, dialogue must do the same.

The dialogue tag

When reading novels by skilled authors, notice how little they rely on dialogue tags; 'he said', 'she said', and so on. When two people are in conversation no such tags should be necessary. One person speaks and the other answers, so if you have established who speaks first, there will be a natural sequence and the reader will easily identify each speaker. And, of course, each new remark will be presented on a new line, as in the following interchange between Joseph Boswell and his illegitimate daughter in *The Mating Dance*.

The daughter is facing her father the morning after a late return from the theatre. He is concerned because her face bears signs of injury. They speak in the slightly 'correct' way of the period. The novel is written in the first person.

'I hope Gavin Calder was not responsible?'

'Gavin! He would never hurt me.'

'Then were you attacked on your way home? Surely you didn't return on foot? You know I will never permit that.'

'We came by hansom, as always, and I suffered no violence anywhere in any way. I tripped over an angle rod backstage and hurt my face. That's all.'

I was now anxious to change the subject; anxious for him to be gone. I wanted no questions about last night.

He said thoughtfully, 'That is what you want me to believe.'

'It is the truth.'

'No. You are hiding something from me, but because it is your wish I will accept your story. Your mother is another matter. She must be cared for.'

'The Steels are doing that. We're staying with them until I can make other arrangements.'

'*You* make other arrangements, a girl barely sixteen!'

'I can find employment.'

'You have it already.'

'A minor player doesn't earn enough for what I intend to do.'

He became angry.

'You heard me say last night that you and Trudy are my responsibility and that I will make arrangements for both of you. I insist on that.'

'I don't consider you have the right.'

'I claim it. I'll find a home for both of you and you will

have the career you were intended for. You will justify the ability you have inherited from me and fulfil all my ambitions for you.' His tone changed. 'I beg you not to disappoint me in this.'

'Surely you don't imagine I could come back to the theatre and continue as a member of the company? There would be embarrassment all round and, besides, Lady Boswell would never agree.'

'It is I who owns the Boswell Theatre and the Boswell Company, and don't forget you have a contract for the part, small though it is. I shall keep you to it. Only the management can terminate a contract, never a player. To enable you to earn more money, you can also understudy the part of Lucie.'

I refused point blank.

'First my mother as your wife's shadow, and now I as your daughter's? Never.'

'That's not how I think of either you or Trudy.'

'It is how *I* feel.'

And now read the same interchange with dialogue tags. To save time, we will pick up the scene half way:

'It is the truth!' I declared vehemently.

'No,' he answered emphatically. 'You are hiding something from me, but because it's your wish I will accept your story. Your mother is another matter. She must be cared for.'

'The Steels are doing that. We are remaining with them until I can make other arrangements,' I retorted triumphantly.

'*You* make other arrangements!' he expostulated. 'A girl barely sixteen!'

'I can find employment,' I flung at him.

'You have that already,' he pointed out angrily.

'A minor player doesn't earn enough for what I intend to do,' I told him resolutely.

At that he became angry. 'You heard me say last night that you and Trudy are my responsibility and that I will make arrangements. I insist on that,' he raged.

'I don't consider you have the right,' I retorted cruelly.

'I claim it,' he shouted furiously.

And so on and so on. An editor would have been itching to delete all those surplus dialogue tags, and if you have managed to read the revised version to the end, you will have been irritated by the unnecessary identification of each speaker and by the repetitive use of adverbs to describe voice tones, all of which were distinguishable by the words they uttered – angry, defensive, emphatic, triumphant, cruel or whatever. In dialogue, let the spoken words speak for themselves and the result will be crisp and clear. Blur them with that enemy of good writing – the superfluous adverb – and their impact will be destroyed. Similarly, too many adjectives to describe nouns are undesirable. There is much truth in the old warning about 'gilding the lily'.

Many new writers wrongly imagine that to use elaborate dialogue tags gives a 'literary' tone to their writing – words like 'ejaculated', 'expostulated', 'protested', 'queried', 'probed', 'avowed', 'declared' and many others gleaned from a favourite thesaurus. Such elaborations are not only unnecessary but jarring because they upset the rhythm of the dialogue. They also make a laboured job of the writing and, in consequence, heavy reading.

Dialogue can be enhanced by correct punctuation and good editing. Why use the word 'exclaimed' when an exclamation mark indicates it (though beware of using these too liberally), and since a question mark is grammatically correct after a question, words like 'asked' or 'queried' or any other indicating a query are unnecessary.

When writing dialogue between more than two people, conditions are slightly different. You will, when necessary, have to indicate who is speaking, particularly when interruptions occur or newcomers join in. Therefore the use of a certain number of dialogue tags will be unavoidable, but use them only when essential and don't waste time in searching for synonyms to replace words like 'said', which identifies a speaker sufficiently when needed. But again, beware – the 'he-said-she-said' syndrome, if overdone, can have as bad a brake action as any other unnecessary dialogue tag.

Direct and indirect dialogue

Creating well balanced dialogue, i.e. between the direct and indirect, is a question of technique and need not be frightening.

Direct dialogue is used when one character talks directly to another, as when relating news or conducting personal conversation – as in the scene where Ruth related her fear to Sylvia.

Indirect dialogue would then be used when Sylvia summarized the news to Peter, after Ruth had gone. It can be employed when the reader already knows past details and repetition is therefore unnecessary. To demonstrate, let's cut into the scene between Ruth and Sylvia and then continue with it, utilising both direct and indirect dialogue.

Example 1: Direct Dialogue:
'. . . Because it sounds insane to say that my husband is trying to have me put away. . .' She reached out and clung to her friend's hands. 'But that is what I believe!'

'My dear – he *wouldn't* ! Whatever makes you think such a thing?'

'He insists that I need a psychiatrist. . . "Long-term psychiatry", he says. I know what that means and it terrifies me. So do the 'phone calls I've been getting. He swears I imagine them. The awful thing is that they're in *his* voice. . . muffled. . .'

The next paragraph continues in direct dialogue because it is necessary for Ruth to relate the circumstances to Sylvia, and at that stage it would be acceptable to readers because they would be interested to know precisely how she would confide in her friend, and how her friend would react. However, if Sylvia then drew Ruth into the living room where Peter was fiddling with the video, repetition would be overloading. It would therefore be necessary to continue the scene like this:

Example 2: Indirect dialogue
'Darling, Ruth's here.' Sylvia stooped and tapped her husband on the shoulder. 'Could you leave that for now? There's something serious. . . something you must hear. . .'

Sensing his wife's concern, Peter looked up. At the sight of Ruth's white face, he reached for the brandy.

'Tell me,' he said.

While he poured, Sylvia repeated what Ruth had told her.

The final line indicates indirect dialogue – i.e. Sylvia's recounting of Ruth's fears. If, however, Sylvia decided to wait until Ruth had gone, she could summarise the situation in direct dialogue with her husband.

On the whole, direct dialogue is preferable to indirect except in the following cases:

(a) When a character must repeat information to another which has already been imparted in direct dialogue (as in *Example 2*).

(b) When a character must explain to another something the reader does not have to learn in detail, such as how to operate a piece of office equipment. (. . . *She showed the new secretary how to surf through the Internet. . .*) Detailed instructions would not enthral the reader (unless already a computer buff), nor would they advance the action. Unless the Internet plays a necessary part in the plot, it may only be there to add to the description of an office background, in which case the mechanics are unimportant.

(c) When long passages of direct dialogue could be broken up, shortened or lightened by the injection of a few lines of indirect dialogue, such as in a scene where a detective is making a verbal report about a case. (. . . *He told Lord William how Lady Dorothy had been traced to Bournemouth, and the circumstances in which she was living with the reprobate Desmond Blake. . .*) The advantages of indirect dialogue are particularly useful in such scenes.

Both direct and indirect dialogue can be used to break up the sort of dénouement scene popular in crime fiction, where the amateur sleuth describes to an assembled company exactly how the crime was committed. (Typical Poirot curtain scenes in Agatha Christie stories.) Questions in direct dialogue could be interchanged with lines of indirect, such as: *The Colonel asked how he first came to suspect the murderer,* then back to the sleuth's revelations in direct dialogue.

Revealing character through dialogue

Up to a point, we reveal ourselves to others whenever we speak. We reveal our thoughts and our moods, our knowledge or lack of it, our sense of humour and our personalities. If we have regional accents, we reveal where we come from. Even our silences can betray us. How many times have you guessed what someone was thinking when they deliberately remained silent?

Pay attention to speech rhythms, pet slang words, accents and dialects but, when using them, don't overdo them. Individual quirks of speech will help to register one character while the frequent use of a particular slang word will characterize another, so that it will only be necessary to introduce these touches to make them instantly recognisable.

Don't force words into their mouths just because you consider them to be clever or witty. The chances are that they may be wholly inappropriate and therefore sound false or out of character.

Now, as an exercise, why not write a dialogue scene between Ruth and her husband Ralph, bringing out his veiled cruelty and her gathering fear and then, as a follow-up, a 'triple' one between Sylvia, Peter, and Ruth? When you have written both, read them aloud or record them and play them back. Both are excellent ways in which to get your ear attuned to realistic dialogue.

Finally, ask yourself this two-part question: Does the dialogue in either scene merely cause it to mark time, like the conversation of the quartet in the coffee shop, or does it advance the story? If you can truthfully answer 'No' to the first and 'Yes' to the second, you are on your way to recognising, and ultimately writing, good fictional conversation.

8. Style and Viewpoint

What is style?

According to many handbooks on the craft of writing, style is a question of approach – first person, third, or 'omniscient' – but part of a lengthy Oxford English Dictionary definition is '. . .manner of writing, speaking, or doing. . . collective characteristics of writing or diction or artistic expression or way of presenting things. . . in the manner of Shakspeare, Raphael, Wagner. . .' None of which teaches us much, except a new way of spelling the Bard's name!

In any case you, the aspiring author with common sense, are not aiming to be the second 'Shakspeare' or the second anybody. Your aim is to be the first You, so that when someone picks up a novel or short story written by you they will recognise your style at once.

Most new authors overwrite. The thought of cutting their work shocks them. All those dedicated hours, all that laboured effort, all that deathless prose laid waste! The thought is positively painful, yet a vast percentage of popular fiction written by aspiring authors could be improved and made marketable by a courageous application of the 'blue pencil'.

The keynote of readability is simplicity. Bog down your reader with over-written narrative and a mass of obscure words and your book will be put aside. Bear in mind that your function as a story teller is to entertain your reader, and how can you do that if you can't tell the story with ease? By that I don't mean casual and slipshod writing; I mean the kind of prose that is simple and direct and seems deceptively easy to write – but there was never a truer saying than 'easy reading is damned hard writing'.

One of the finest exponents of this style was Ernest Hemingway. Read *The Old Man and The Sea*. It contains not one over-elaborate sentence and it ranks among the greats.

I am not saying that good prose should not contain vivid metaphors or similes (though the simile needs to be good if it is not to appear contrived), but if a novel contains so many that they seem to occur in every other paragraph the style can become wearisome and act as an obstacle to readability. Nor, in contrast, am I saying that your fiction should be as matter-of-fact as journalism which, even at its best, is written mainly for factual communication. Nor am I saying that novels containing clichés, contrived similes, and laboured metaphors don't get published. We have all, at some time or other, struggled to read such books and put them aside.

What I *am* saying is: Don't handicap your novel by trying to be clever, or trying to impress some unknown reader with your vocabulary and your skill in using it. In the process you may well lose sight of your main objective – to tell a story. Bear in mind that your job, as novelist or short story teller, is to do precisely that; and the more simply and directly you do it, the more readable your story will be.

Approach, ancient and modern

Since approach is an important part of style, let's now examine the three main ones, starting with the omniscient.

In this style you play God, talking down to your readers, forecasting what is to come, writing in the present tense and introducing your characters almost with a running commentary accompanied by interjections and much sermonizing. The Victorians loved it and presented it in this way:

> Amelia hurries down the darkening lane, clutching her sweeping skirts in one trembling hand and her valise in the other, her guilty heart racing in time with her frantic steps. Oh, how wicked she has been to run away! Such behaviour is always disgraceful in a well brought up young lady, as you and I know, gentle reader. She must now go back and face whatever penance her sin so rightly deserves, but alas, she has lost her way and gathering fog now obscures her vision! Then suddenly her heart lifts, for out of the darkness looms the shadow of a house. Oh, merciful promise of shelter on this woeful night!
>
> But poor Amelia is mistaken. Little does she dream of what lies ahead. Pity her, dear reader, for the shock and distress in store, and pray that courage will sustain her.

You may argue that no author writes that way today, but many aspiring ones touch the fringe of it. Unconsciously, they adapt it to modern idiom, often retaining the present tense so popular with the Victorians. Study the next example and you will see what I mean.

> The car engine splutters, dies, and refuses to come alive. Furiously, Martin seizes his suitcase and begins to walk. He feels guilty for slamming the door on his parents after the row about his association with Ruby. Just because she'd been divorced twice didn't mean there would be a third time. All the same, he shouldn't have behaved like that. He must go back and talk over the whole thing reasonably and quietly. He must make amends, as his regrettable behaviour so rightly demands, for no son should treat his parents in such a fashion.
>
> The breakdown of his car is frustrating, but he recalls driving over a level crossing a short time ago, which means that a train service should not be too far distant. And he is right – or so he thinks. He can see a huddle of buildings which he takes to be a station, but little does he dream how wrong he is. It would have been wiser to search for a garage to repair his car, but of course he does not know that yet. Nor can he envisage the nightmare lying in wait for him.

This foreshadowing of events may be preferable to the rambling writing of earlier days, but it still jars and the author's Victorian-style interjections and sermonising are not only obtrusive but irritating.

Such a style is unacceptable today. It can be called 'the seeing eye' or even the 'judicial omniscient', both of which make for bad writing and worse reading. Even so, varied samples continue to land on the desks of fiction editors, usually in travel-weary typescripts.

Enough of the omniscient, seeing-eye and foreshadowing styles, and on to the next logical step.

Third person 'limited' and third person 'straight'

In some ways third person 'limited' can be an extension of the omniscient, but with no interpolations, no sermonising, and no stage asides. The author writes from a grandstand seat, but he is not there to make a commentary so again his voice must never be heard. Because he stays with the main character throughout, usually the hero or heroine, he relates the story entirely from that character's point of view, thus limiting it. It is a device to win exclusive sympathy for the leading character.

This single-minded approach is akin to the normal (or 'straight') third person, but is much more restrictive. In the latter the author ostensibly focuses on the central character, but has the advantage of getting within the skin of all other characters and moving with them from scene to scene instead of remaining doggedly with the hero. He is therefore able to present their thoughts and actions as well as the leading character's. This form of third person approach is a popular method of story-telling and therefore the most used, but it has its dangers as well as its advantages.

Apart from being able to switch from character to character and from place to place, there is the advantage of being able to open a new scene with a different person each time, or resurrecting one who bowed out earlier but who can now be useful in engineering a dramatic turn in events. This gives the author a welcome breather and avoids the likelihood of being stuck in a rut, wondering how to get out of it. It also enables him to reveal off-stage behaviour and dialogue, *but* it also lures an inexperienced writer into one specific danger, that of leaping from the thoughts and actions of one character to another in scenes which should focus only on the character occupying centre stage.

Jumping from character to character and from mind to mind *within* a scene will destroy that scene. Here is an example:

As James paced the floor, waiting for Helen to arrive, he was conscious of the threadbare carpet, the shabby room, the spluttering gas fire which indicated that the fifty pence he had put in the meter was running out and, dear God, what would he do if it ran out completely and the room was frozen by the time she came? He couldn't spare another fifty so soon. As for his shoes, he hoped the polish he had diligently applied would disguise their shabbiness and that the careful pressing he had given his suit would do the same. It would be galling if she were to guess how things were with him now.

When he opened the door, she stared. She looked beyond him to the depressing bed-sitter. She frowned on the cheap curtains and the stained wallpaper. She could even detect a sort of fading, gassy smell as if one of those awful spluttery fires had just died. And as for James, his cuffs were frayed and his shoes shabby. He looked down on his luck. Well, well, well. . . who'd have expected a man like James to sink to this?

James smiled nervously. He wished she had never traced him. He felt humiliated and ashamed and hated her for it. He wanted to tell her to go. He wanted to slam the door in her face. He couldn't. He could only step aside for her to enter.

I wrote that to demonstrate how continuity was destroyed by switching from the inside of James's mind (paragraph 1) to the inside of Helen's (paragraph 2) and back again to his (paragraph 3). The whole scene should have been enacted through *his* mind and *his* eyes because in that scene he was the central character. Not until it was over should I have switched to Helen, writing the next one from her point of view. I could then have shown her walking away down the street and, putting myself into her mind, revealed her compassion and her anxiety to help him without hurting his pride. All this would come through her thoughts and she would emerge as a more sympathetic character.

First person singular

There is a common belief that writing in the first person singular is restrictive. I have heard teachers of creative writing, who should know better, issue it as a warning to new writers, discouraging them before they even try it.

'It's no use writing fiction in the first person because you can't reveal the thoughts and feelings of other characters that way. And you can't relate what's going on elsewhere because the 'I' person can't possibly know. You can only convey all that in third person.' Those words were once spoken at a writers' seminar by a woman novelist and TV personality who, apparently, was unacquainted with any books but her own.

From where did these misguided theories come? Who first created this bogey to frighten an aspiring author who instinctively wants to write in the first person and is now too afraid to try? It certainly didn't come from the hundreds of successful authors, both past and present, who have used the first person for books that have won worldwide fame. Their number is legion.

Take Charlotte Brontë's *Jane Eyre* for a start, a novel involving a host of characters whose actions, both on and off stage, are vital to the story's development. And how about Robert Louis Stevenson's *Kidnapped* and *Catriona?* Or Wilkie Collins's *The Woman in White?* What about *David Copperfield* – how did Dickens write *that* immortal tale?

Nearer our own time, Daphne du Maurier showed us how to do it in those unforgettable novels, *Rebecca, My Cousin Rachel,* and *The Scapegoat.* Could the last one have been written in any other way, and could the first one have had a more haunting opening line than, 'Last night I dreamt I went to Manderley again. . .'? (*What* an opening, enticing the reader to accompany the voice along that ancient, neglected drive. . .)

And did the readers of any of these books fail to sense or suspect the thoughts and feelings of other characters? In *Rebecca,* Max de Winter's turmoiled emotions, and the smouldering enmity of Mrs Danvers toward the very ordinary young woman who had replaced her late and beloved mistress, were conveyed strongly through the heroine's first-person narrative. Emotional tension, personal conflict, and individual reactions crackled from the pages – and all their voices and guarded words were wholly revealing to the reader.

And what of Hammond Innes's yarns, all written in the first person, teeming with varied characters and alive with action? Desmond Bagley did it, too, and so have many, many others, but perhaps Susan Howatch has made the method distinctly her own.

For her, writing exclusively in the first person is obviously vital. Neither length nor time lapses daunt her. The 1,090 pages of *The Wheel of Fortune*, the panoramic sagas of *Penmarric* and *Cashelmara*, the lengthy pageantry of *Glittering Images* and its successors – all these and others of her books should be read and re-read by those who maintain that writing in the first person should be avoided.

In lighter vein, but confirming the effectiveness of the first person approach, Mary Stewart's romantic suspense novels still retain, for many, the popularity they won in the 1950s, and for really brilliant first person writing read Thomas Hinde's *The Day The Call Came.* If you know the novel already you cannot fail to remember the important role of the narrator's wife, who never appears in the book but whose concern for her husband's sanity becomes increasingly evident until she brings about the climax of the story – but it is *he* who tells the tale.

As for conveying the secret thoughts and plans of other characters in a first person story, we have only to turn to Robert Louis Stevenson's *Kidnapped*. Remember David Balfour's arrival at the house called Shaws, to the surprise of old Ebenezer? From dialogue and character portrayal the reader guesses that the old man plans to get rid of the boy, but David doesn't have a suspicion until Ebenezer sends him up that unfinished staircase in total darkness. Not until the boy reaches the terrifying drop does he realise his danger, but readers sense it long before that.

We, as readers, are onlookers seeing most of the game. This gives the 'first person' author a big advantage, for not only do we listen to every remark and every response and interpret them exactly as the author intended us to, but the personal involvement draws us deeper into the characters' minds until we can anticipate how they are going to feel or react in given situations.

In this way we sensed that young Balfour's innocence and trust were tools old Ebenezer was using to lure him up that perilous staircase and to hold us, the readers, in a state of suspicion and apprehension. From the start, we had been drawn into a well woven first-person net which third-person narration could not have bettered.

Could that staircase scene in *Kidnapped* have been written in third person? Undoubtedly, but would it have been so effective? We would have been *shown* the boy groping his way in the dark, but would not have climbed the stairs *with* him, sharing the experience both as onlooker and participator. And in third person it would have been easy to switch to the old man's triumphant thoughts, giving the game away prematurely. Robert Louis Stevenson was plainly aware that, in this instance, first person singular imparted a greater sense of immediacy than third person would have done.

Two-character responses in first-person treatment

To answer the question of how to convey, in first person, the thoughts of two people when each is ignorant of the other's, turn to *Jane Eyre* and study the memorable garden scene, with Mr Rochester pretending to be unaware of Jane's presence while she sits quietly sewing, eyes downcast, praying that he will not notice her but longing for him to do so. Told exclusively by her, we are not only aware of his approach but why he is taking his time over it, pausing to examine a bush here, a flower there, never glancing toward her. We know exactly what is in his mind, while she is totally unaware of it. Read that scene and you will absorb the skill of first-person writing and the dual emotions charging it.

A first-person problem which does need to be mastered is that of conveying events which have taken place offstage; events the 'I' person has not witnessed but which must be revealed. It is all a question of communication. Remember that communication is a two-way thing; you receive it and you impart it. You talk to people and they talk to you. You listen, question, search, and you receive information, news, items of gossip. All this propels a story forward, whatever its tense, and it must be natural, easy, flowing. . .

'My dear, you should have been here when Mabel and John called. What *do* you think happened?'

Out pours the news, the picture takes shape, the narrator does a U-turn and the story leaps ahead.

Or someone could burst into a scene, conveying news in a way which also tells us a lot about the speaker and why she has arrived.

The last person I expected to see, when I answered the door, was Brenda Forsythe. 'So glad you're in,' she said, strolling into the living room in that lazy way of hers. 'I missed you at Steve's house-warming last night. Did you forget, or some-thing? Y'know, I thought you and he were just like *that*. . . .' She held up two fingers, close together. 'Anyway, it was a pity you missed it because who d'you think dropped in? Your dear Uncle James. It was plain as a pikestaff why he was there – to drag his darling daughter away, your sweet little coz, Daphne. Oh yes, she was there – wouldn't you have expected her to be? No – I thought perhaps you mightn't. . . anyway, there she was and having a whale of a time. I must say her dear Papa showed an admirable restraint. After downing a drink, he congratulated Steve on the way he'd done up the place and said, "Get her back to the students' hostel by eleven, won't you?" and took his leave. We all fell about laughing then, because everyone knows – except you, perhaps? – that dear little Daph quit the hostel a week ago and shacked up with Steve. Perhaps that's why you didn't turn up, darling? Oh dear, have I said the wrong thing?'

I didn't answer. I couldn't. When she strolled to the door I let her see herself out.

There is no need to say more in a scene like that. The main character, the 'I' person, has placed you, the reader, as watcher in the third corner of the triangle, so you know well enough what she is thinking and feeling *and* the malicious satisfaction of her visitor.

For a modern story there are many forms of communication, some of which are trite but nonetheless essential in our lives and therefore acceptable in fiction. There is the unpredictable telephone with its ability to ring at crucial moments; there is the news flash on TV or car radio; there is the unexpected letter that shocks or delights. All are legitimate forms of communication and can be used as advantageously in first person as in third.

Even the long arm of coincidence can, *if handled well*, be used convincingly from any viewpoint but, unless it is unavoidable, try not to drag in the conveniently overheard conversation. The fact that in real life we we overhear people talking in shops, buses, adjoining offices or elsewhere, does not make it easily acceptable in fiction. To have someone deliberately listening to a private conversation, from behind a half open door, smacks of dishonesty, like reading other people's letters. Your bad characters can do it. Your good ones can't.

Another first person singular problem which worries aspiring authors is how to depict the 'I' person's looks. They argue that you can't have a heroine boasting that she is pretty, or describing her features in detail. True. So you do it in other ways, as in the following extract from an early novel of mine.

Unlike myself, my mother had been a beauty, but she had passed on to me at least a measure of her looks, plus her tall slender figure. I had in my possession a miniature which my father always carried, painted when she was twenty, a year older than I am now. From it her large grey eyes, set beneath eyebrows that looked as if they had been stroked in by an artist's brush, conveyed humour and honesty and warmth. Her face was oval and her smooth hair was braided into a coronet. I had adopted this style instinctively when the time came for me to put up my hair and I could well remember coming downstairs, standing before my father, and seeing his start of surprise. Then his kindly eyes had filled with unexpected tears.

All he said was, 'You are so like her, it seems almost untrue. God has been good to let her live again in you.'

(From: *The Arrogant Duke*)

The passage conveys more than the heroine's appearance. It reveals the love her parents had shared, her father's pride in his daughter, and the girl's modesty ('Unlike myself, my mother had been a beauty. . .').

In any genre and in any approach, useful information can be conveyed indirectly. The fact that she had reached the age 'to put up her hair' conveniently indicated that the story was a period one.

Mirrors are unfailingly useful, whatever the gender and whatever the viewpoint, but particularly so in first person singular. Being an essential part of our lives, it doesn't smack of conceit when characters catch sight of themselves and react accordingly. A Regency dandy can inspect the tying of his high cravat and, in his thoughts, express his dissatisfaction and his resolve to reprimand his valet, thereby revealing both his vanity and his pettiness. An ageing woman can catch a glimpse of wrinkles and sagging contours and mentally sigh for the days of her youth. 'Thank God he can't see me now! I want him to remember me as I was.' And a modern young woman can give voice to her reaction in this way:

Heavens, what a mess I looked, with my red hair scraped back to keep it out of my eyes, smudges on my face, soil on my jeans, not even a comb handy for a quick repair job and chunky clothes making me look more tubby than ever! The reflection was thrown back at me from the greenhouse windows as he came striding along the path, saying he'd been ringing the front door bell without success so had come round the side to look for me. Why are other women never caught at their worst? Why couldn't *I* have been born a natural beauty who looks lovely even without make-up?

There is more than just a woman's appearance there. There is consternation because she has been caught at a bad moment by a man whose reactions are obviously important to her. First person viewpoint can convey vital touches as effortlessly as any other.

And, again from any viewpoint but of particular use in first person, critical relatives can draw attention to a person's looks. A proud mother can remark on her daughter's loveliness when dressed for a party, or comment adversely on her make-up or on such things as artificial highlights which, in her opinion, mar the girl's chestnut hair. A father can growl his disapproval of a son's way-out gear, his terse comments painting an immediate vignette. Similarly, the briefest remarks can indicate an underlying attitude or emotion.

How, for instance, would you make a man reveal against his will, to a woman who angers him, that underneath it all she attracts him? Mary Stewart did it long ago in *Madam, Will You Talk?* The heroine is kidnapping a child with the father in hot pursuit. (She has wrong ideas about his motives, of course, but we have not.) At length he catches up with her and, in a towering rage, he blazes, 'You beautiful bitch!'

Leave out the word beautiful and you have a man who hates her. Put it in and it reveals how he really sees her despite his rage, but because *she* is hating *him* she doesn't heed the adjective. Only to the reader does it speak volumes.

First person detached

When writing from this viewpoint, the narrator does not necessarily have to be the central character. This is especially useful when observing and commenting on others.

If you feel you can tell the story more effectively through the mind of someone else, such as a son telling his father's story and the scandal or political drama that made the man notorious, or a mother telling the story of her daughter's rise to fame and fortune, or a sister revealing the reverse side of a picture hitherto accepted by everyone, then you will have the advantage of ready accessibility to scenes both on and off stage; a bird's eye view of all situations and events.

This can best be described as an extension of the first person viewpoint. It is popular in historical fiction, enabling the author to use an imaginary character – a servant, steward, or lady's maid – to relate a fictionalized version of events in contrast with recorded history; a sort of eye-witness account which would have been unheeded had such a lowly witness actually lived.

But remember that when using the voice of an onlooker, skilful writing is required to steer the reader's self-identification to the right quarter and to keep it there throughout the novel. One of the best examples of this approach is Bamber Gascoigne's *The Heyday*. In this novel a young man tells the story of his Edwardian grandmother in the brilliance of her theatrical prime. He never knew her. She has long been dead, but she is the central character throughout, not merely as an undying legend but as a living, breathing, vital person brought alive by the 'I' voice of her unknown grandson. Read it, enjoy it, and learn.

Now try it yourself

As a triple exercise, take the long-lost Elspeth Marshall from Chapter 3 and visualise her return to her native village. Decide at which point you will start; with her actual arrival, with the meeting of mother and daughter, or with a confrontation between Elspeth and the currently official Mrs Marshall at The White Horse. Then write the scene (a) in third person, (b) in first person, and (c) in first person detached (for which you will have to find the voice of an onlooker – such as an old school friend, or an employee at the inn, or a long-standing village gossip – a further exercise for your imagination).

When you have written all three, you will know in which viewpoint you feel most at ease. It will be the one in which you are anxious to continue writing.

When you have finished, try writing it from other angles. It will be good practice, and comparing the different results will not only be interesting but will also demonstrate the effectiveness, or otherwise, of each approach. It will also confirm which is the right one for *you*.

9. Construction

Working to a blue print – or not?

A frequent question from aspiring authors to published ones, is whether they write in longhand or use a keyboard.

Now we are on trickier ground. If I confess that I write 'straight out of my head' – which I do once I have a strong awareness of my lead character and immediate supporting ones, and one or two possible situations involving them, or an opening paragraph hammering in my mind – there is the danger that new writers will assume mine to be the correct way of working and that they are not being truly creative unless they do the same.

To me, there is no 'correct' way of working other than the one which comes instinctively, so again my answer must be 'the choice is yours', but with certain qualifications.

If you have a writing tutor who advises you to work to a detailed synopsis, stay with it as long as you work confidently and happily that way, but when you are alone with your pile of blank paper or empty screen, don't be afraid to try another approach if you feel the urge to.

If you find sticking to an outline difficult and that you wander away from it as your story grows, don't worry – this can be a very good sign, indicating that your imagination is working well, that it is taking control. This is commonly regarded as working by inspiration, but it is really your 'subconscious' playing its part, as with my 'inspired' picture of the Edwardian mother and daughter who ultimately led me to *Dragonmede*.

We have already established that the subconscious mind is a storehouse of facts and fancies, of forgotten experiences and impressions and thoughts and questions, all of which start surfacing when the conscious mind takes a rest. When these moments of inspiration come, seize them and store them, as I stored that mother and daughter. As your storehouse grows, jot down notes as memory-joggers. From these you can create an outline, building up a detailed plot if you feel you can work better that way.

Whether you decide to produce a blue print or not, you will be in good company. The late John Braine once told me that he always made a chapter-by-chapter outline and that Arnold Bennett did the same. I used to regard the fact that I do not as a personal idiosyncracy and was relieved to learn that many professional authors work as I do, including Stan Barstow who, in an interview, admitted that he was content to start from scratch and that with only the vaguest ideas he was prepared to write a couple of sentences and follow a thread which, months later, 'led him out at the end of the novel'. In contrast, the French crime writer, Georges Simenon, never started a novel without first drawing up a detailed blue print.

While it seems reasonable that the intricacies of crime fiction should demand this method more than would a wholly emotional story, another crime writer, Marion Babson — a winner of the Crime Writers' Association's accolade for the libraries' most borrowed crime writer — admits that with only certain incidents and the crime's solution in mind she starts from scratch and that she would experience less enjoyment otherwise.

There is a well known story about a highly successful American author of the sixties and seventies whose publisher, visiting him one day, saw a sheet of paper in his typewriter, stooped to read what was on it, found it exciting and promptly asked what was to happen next. 'I don't know,' said this top-selling author. 'My typewriter has broken down.'

I relate this story only to demonstrate that every author will eventually find his or her own method of working, usually by a process of trial and error. Individuality being the nature of authorship, it stands to reason that no hard and fast rules regarding working methods can be laid down.

However, guidance *can* be offered, for example on the construction of character dossiers and on overcoming certain technical difficulties; also on the presentation of manuscripts and the marketing of fiction (see Chapter 12), but the best working method for *you* is something only you will eventually discover. You may draw up dozens of plot outlines, only to find that when you get down to work your imagination takes control and you forget or ignore the lot of them. Words either spring into your mind and take you with them, or you stare at a blank sheet of paper and then reach thankfully for your blue print. Either way can prove to be the best for *you*.

What I want to do is to free you from restriction, from any rigid ideas regarding the 'right' and the 'wrong' way to work. Most textbooks on the craft of writing advocate the use of a plot outline, sometimes to the extent of turning it into a laborious job guaranteed to quench an author's enthusiasm long before he even thinks of an opening line. One American textbook even devotes the bulk to what the author apparently considers an infallible method of plot building, a complex jigsaw to be completed before even a word of the novel is put down on paper.

The method consists of taking a large ringed looseleaf book and dividing it into manifold sections, each marked with gummed tabs. *Calendar* is the first section, followed by another labelled *Timing*; the first, for noting the dates on which work is carried out and the second, for recording the number of hours devoted to it (all of which could be jotted down in one's diary equally well). Still more sub-divisions must be headed *Plotting Begun* and *Plotting Finished*, for insertion of dates; *Estimated Length*; *Chapters*; *Chapter Pages* (with sample calculations such as '20 chapters, 15 pages each = 300 pages', disregarding the necessity for chapters to end only at a climactic or suspenseful moment, which alone dictates their length).

And that is not all. Still more sections should be labelled *Situations, Development of Situations*; *Outcome of Developments*; *Chronology*; *Titles*; *Theme*; *Plotting*; *Plotting Twists*; *Characters*; *Character Types*; *Character Names*; *Character Reactions*; *Character Situations*. . . all designed to force a beginner's mind on to complicated tracks.

I put it to the test with a plot from one of my own books, dissecting it according to the specifications, only to find (as I expected) that filling a large, record book with innumerable divisions devoted to so many specific headings resulted in a lot of unnecessary duplications. For example, the sections *Situations, Development of Situations,* and *Outcome of Situations,* being interrelated to the point of being indivisible, therefore had to be slotted into all relevant sections and the same applied to almost every other aspect.

As a way of devising a complex Chinese puzzle I can think of no better method, so here let me sound a warning: don't bog yourself down with too much theorising. Don't place reliance on clever tricks. Ignore advertisements for ready made plots 'Guaranteed To Sell Your Stories' (they won't) or to others guaranteeing to lead you to bestsellerdom overnight (*they* won't either).

And don't create a convoluted Spaghetti Junction of any outline you make. Keep it to essentials. You may find it quite sufficient to jot down reminders of forthcoming crises in the story as you currently visualise them, despite the likelihood of these events yielding to others as the book progresses. If you wish, and if you feel it keeps a goal in sight, you can also plan the end, but don't be surprised if that also changes before you reach it.

Constant change and unexpected developments are aspects of fiction writing that make it surprising and challenging and enjoyable, so don't worry if your blue print isn't strictly adhered to. How often have you veered away from a road map *en route* to a destination and found it to be a better route than the one you planned?

Releasing the creative process

It is an undoubted fact that it is only when one is actually writing that one becomes truly creative. You may embark on a novel with only a minimal idea in your head, or perhaps an opening paragraph, or a scene which you think will come somewhere in midstream, or a beginning which you know will lead you somewhere, or an ending which shines like a light at the end of a tunnel. You may anticipate no problems at all from a carefully worked out plot, but the fact remains that at whatever stage you start to write, your story will only come to life once you start putting words down on paper. That is when creativity takes over and the real work starts.

The hours you devote to writing must depend on your personal circumstances; whether you have household or family responsibilities, or a daily job which you cannot afford to give up until you become well established as an author (and even then it is not always wise to). Whatever your situation, you must adapt your writing time to the demands of your lifestyle, but one thing I do advise – make a point of writing something every day, at whatever moment you can squeeze it in, whether in the train on your way to and from work, or when the children are at school, or during the evening while the family watches television. If you can fit in this session at the same time every day, so much the better. It will then become a habit as necessary to you as breathing.

I cannot emphasize strongly enough the value of a daily writing stint, even if it bears no relation to a story in its embryonic state. Write *anything*, and you will find that even when you think you are tired or uninspired, words will come and sentences will form and fatigue will slowly yield to creativity. Simultaneously, you will establish the habit of self-discipline, vital to every author.

But when finally sitting down to write that fictional work you have long been mulling over, you will find that you come face to face with certain structural problems, all of which have to be tackled and which all writers have to master. Let's take them one by one.

The narrative hook

This is not to be confused with the dialogue hook, but it performs the same function. In case you are unfamiliar with the term, it is used to describe an opening sentence, paragraph, or scene designed to grab the reader's attention and to provoke his curiosity to such a degree that he is compelled to read on.

Such a hook is desirable, even essential, at the start of a story. It can be startling, shocking, frightening, amusing or simply intriguing and, for preference, it should also convey some interesting or provocative information about the central character or characters, as a sort of appetizer whetting the reader's desire to learn about them.

A fine example is the opening to Susan Howatch's novel, *The Rich Are Different*:

> I was in London when I first heard of Dinah Slade. She was broke and looking for a millionaire while I was rich and looking for a mistress. From the start we were deeply compatible.

Apart from the concise wit and the intriguing situation presented in those economical lines, they also convey some vivid character portrayal. We know at once that he is ruthless as well as rich, selfish as well as shrewd; a man wanting to buy a mistress either because he shirks the responsibility of a wife or because he has one already, and his shrewdness sparks his quick assessment of

Dinah Slade. Through his succinct observation we recognise the cold calculation of her and, because of it, we know she will be well able to hold her own. So there they are, the pair of them, ready to use each other without scruple. Compatible? Only as far as characteristics go and, for that reason, plainly in line for a head-on clash.

As readers, we find such a clever narrative hook intriguing. How will two such people make out? What happens next? We can't wait to discover.

For a chilling and challenging opening paragraph to a chilling and disturbing story, let's take the opening to Dean Koontz's *Strangers*.

Dominick Corvaisis went to sleep under a light wool blanket and a crisp white sheet, sprawled alone in his bed, but he woke elsewhere – in the darkness of a large foyer closet, behind concealing coats and jackets. He was curled in the foetal position. His hands were squeezed into tight fists. The muscles in his neck and arms ached from a bad though unremembered dream.

He could not recall leaving the comfort of his mattress during the night, but he was not surprised to find that he had travelled in the dark hours. It had happened on two other occasions, and recently.

Where is he? How did he get into that clothes cupboard? Why the foetal position and the clenched hands? How did he travel in the dark hours without being aware of it? Our curiosity is whetted because this is plainly no ordinary case of sleep-walking. A shiver of expectancy is immediately stirred, impossible to resist.

In contrast, Thomas Hinde's opening to *Agent*, described in the press as 'a thriller-plus' and 'a bleak allegorical nightmare', grips the reader in an entirely different way. Here is the opening:

Lena is coming tonight.

She does mimes for me. Right in the middle of one she'll burst into tears, though she won't show it. She'll keep her face turned away from me, trying to hide them, continuing her act, but I'll catch glimpses of her crumpled face and see flashes of light reflected in the drops on it. Things have happened to Lena which should never have happened to a girl of her age – what a mistaken thought. It's because of what's happened to her that I so admire her.

What things have happened to her? What experiences are hidden behind her brave front? Who is she? And why does she come to this man (you know instinctively that the narrator is male) to do mimes for him, and at night? A narrative hook like that is irresistible because Lena is irresistible.

I said earlier that the narrative hook could also be amusing and provocative. That such an opening could seize a reader's immediate attention was proved as long ago as 1796 when Jane Austin began to write *Pride and Prejudice*:

> It is a truth universally acknowledged, that a single man in possession of good fortune must be in want of a wife.

It needs no more than that pithy observation to plunge the reader into the fluttering excitement of ambitious Mamas and the coquettish rivalry of their daughters; no more than that to entertain and intrigue. Readers have been caught by that opening paragraph since it first appeared in print in 1813.

Four differing narrative hooks, and all successful.

A rewarding exercise, which can serve the dual purpose of stimulating your imagination and sparking further ideas for stories as well as training you in the art of writing good narrative hooks, is to write as many challenging beginnings as you can think of. Let them come out of the top of your head, giving no thought to tying them up with any story you may currently have in mind; in fact, the less they are associated with any specific piece of work the better, and highly desirable at this stage. You are doing this exercise for the combined purposes of mastering the narrative hook and of jerking your mind into action. Out of the medley you produce, at least one hook is likely to seize your imagination, spurring you into creativity and a resultant story.

The chapter hook

This applies to chapter endings, when the curtain must descend at a point so dramatic or thought-provoking that readers are compelled to read on. This does not mean that every chapter break must be sensational or violent or melodramatic; it can finish on a note of emotional conflict, or on one of question or doubt, but suspense of some kind *must* be maintained to whet the reader's interest.

The technique is identical to that used in drama. The curtain must descend at a point where the audience will be agog for it to rise again, so again I recommend that you read as many successful plays as possible. You will then recognise the value of surprise or shock or fear or bewilderment followed by the 'quick cut', to be followed by more until the final curtain descends with all the questions answered and all loose ends tidied off, leaving the audience satisfied or justifiably *dis*satisfied if the ending is disappointing and flat. The same technique applies to story-telling. The reader's curiosity must be held until the close of the final chapter; if not, you have failed as a story teller.

Chapter lengths

While on the subject of chapters, I must dispel a belief which seems to be common among new writers; namely, that chapters should be divided numerically, i.e. fifteen pages per chapter, or some similar fixed number. I even saw a letter published on the readers' page of a writers' magazine, written by a self-congratulatory beginner, describing how she had 'hit on an excellent method of chapter control' by dividing her sheaf of typing paper into batches of fifteen sheets, so that when she reached the end of the last one she knew she had completed another chapter. 'In that way,' she continued, 'you don't have to wonder when to end a chapter.'

I wanted to advise her not only to study more published novels, but also the chapter hooks of successful ones. She would then have learned that length does *not* control chapter endings, that curtains must rise and fall only when the right, suspenseful moment dictates (as already stressed under *The chapter hook* above). Too early or too late or at numerically regulated intervals, regardless of tension or suspended conflict, will not only make the story fall flat, but guarantee that the reader won't bother to turn the pages.

An expert handler of chapter hooks is the American author, Mary Higgins Clark, whom every writer should study, not only for the quality of her writing but for the quality of her stories and her highly individual approach to construction. The only factor governing chapter endings in her novels is the *story*, whether chapters are long or short or as brief as an episode. Her narrative hooks are brilliant and the descent of her chapter curtains immaculately timed. Read *The Cradle Will Fall, Caribbean Blues,* and *All Around The Town* for starters. Enjoy and learn.

Transitions

One of the more worrying problems for new writers, and one of the easiest to handle, is the transition; how to bridge gaps in time, how to transport characters from place to place or from scene to scene. Such situations are unavoidable in any story.

Bear in mind that transitions serve two useful functions; they help to keep the action moving and they increase readability by contributing to a smooth and flowing style. Let's write a bad transition and then analyse just why it is bad. We'll go back to Chapter 7 and Ruth's visit to her friend, Sylvia.

> Once she had made up her mind, Ruth decided to call on Sylvia without delay. Opening the hall cupboard, she seized her coat blindly, shrugged into it and set out to walk, thinkng that to do so, rather than drive, would help to calm her down. Today, however, the distance seemed longer than usual because she was impatient to get there, impatient to seek her friends' reassurance and help. Along Heathfield Road she walked, turned right into the seemingly endless stretch of Mulberry Lane, and began to wish she had driven after all. At last she reached the turning where Sylvia lived, but as she approached the house apprehension seized her. What if she was making a mistake? What if both Sylvia and Peter refused to believe her?
>
> Momentarily, she faltered, then resolutely walked on. With the same resolute step she approached their front door and rang the bell. Even then she was tempted to turn back, but the door was opened immediately and Sylvia stood there.
>
> 'Ruth, how nice to see you! Come along in. I was thinking of you only today. . .'

The meeting could then follow as written, but its impact would be weaker through over-writing. Such a clumsy and lengthy transition holds up the action because it adds nothing. There is no need to follow a character from place to place, or to describe in detail how they get there, unless something happens *en route* which affects the story.

Compare the foregoing with the following:

Once she had made up her mind, Ruth called on Sylvia without delay. She was glad when her friend promptly answered the door because it gave her no time to hesitate or withdraw. *(The scene then proceeds as written.)*

Scene should immediately follow scene without any surplus prose acting as a brake between them. And remember that your readers don't want or need to be led by the hand. If it is written well, they can grasp a situation and visualise a scene without any unnecessary elaboration. Retard the action with trivial details and excess wordage, and their interest, like the story, will flag.

Bridging the gap

Another effective way of handling a transition is to insert a gap in the narrative. This is commonly known as a 'space break' and is particularly useful in indicating time switches. In Ruth's case we could use it in the following way, changing her method of approach.

To make sure that Sylvia would be in, Ruth telephoned her.
'May I pop round to see you?' she asked. 'I'd like to talk.'
'My dear, I'd be delighted. Come at once – we haven't had a good natter for ages !'
Ten minutes later, Ruth was ringing the doorbell.

. . . and the scene continues as before.

See how simple it is to handle transitions? There is no need to be afraid of them or to try to dodge them. Make them serve you as effectively as they are designed to, and they will cease to be bogies.

The flashback

As a reader, I find nothing more 'off-putting' than slices of badly handled retrospection. Flashbacks are often useful, sometimes essential, but very often used as a means of escape from a situation which is proving difficult to handle. To indulge in the reminiscent thoughts of a character offers a convenient way out while seeking a solution to a problem, but the reader may well feel frustrated if, at a moment when he is expecting the story to move forward, he finds it going backward. If this is indulged in too often, without advancing the tale, he will put the book aside and be unlikely to pick it up again.

When that happens, the flashback has been badly handled. It should never mark time, never be a hold-up. Like everything else in the writing of popular fiction, the flashback should help to advance the story, never to retard it. That is why it is so difficult to use. Marching backward never advances anyone's footsteps, but retracing a few steps can achieve a detour which will bring them out at a point further ahead. That is what the well handled flashback does.

When writing my trilogy of novels about the Drayton pottery family, I was faced with the enormous problem of bridging gaps between the generations without repeating large slices of information with which earlier readers would already be acquainted. (I will touch on this in more detail in Chapter 11, on the writing of sequels.) It was essential, in developing the character of the last-born Drayton son, to reveal resemblances to his dead father *and* to the circumstances of his father's death, although it happened before the son was born.

Since the past influenced the present, certain revelations had to be made. To actually re-live them retrospectively meant jumping back into the previous book, with consequent repetition and no advancement in the sequel; so the obvious method was to filter hints through the medium of the son's thoughts when he occasionally recalled veiled references to his father's death, through his consequent curiosity, and through the conversations of other characters when, observing his own behaviour, they remarked on his resemblance to his father and recollected certain past episodes.

This method served the purpose of awakening the reader's interest in the past, throwing light on unanswered questions, and arousing curiosity about the present.

That is the value of the flashback. It can also be valuable in portraying nostalgia, such as a woman's longing for a vital moment in her past or a turning point in her life which is suddenly recalled by a reminder of some kind – such as a musical strain, or a drift of perfume.

To me, one of the most evocative garden scents is that of mignonette, a border plant originally cultivated at the time of the Civil War. It is a modest plant, its small clusters of pale flowers so unremarkable that it was ultimately regarded as a weed and fell from favour. However, when visiting the grounds of a National Trust country house one day I caught its fragrance and was carried back to my childhood home and the clumps growing wildly in the small garden. It inspired a flashback in a story I was then writing about a young woman whose village lover was away fighting for the Roundheads.

Dutifully tending her mother's garden one evening, the perfume of mignonette revived in her memory the moment when he had proposed to her, and their ensuing secrecy because her parents would have opposed the marriage. The flashback served the purpose far better than a trite recitation of facts lacking any nostalgia or emotional depth.

To handle a short flashback well, it is important to keep it confined. This is commonly known as 'framing' and it means restricting it within the immediate moment and then, at the end of the flashback, reverting to the same moment as if it had never been interrupted.

In other words, you don't leave the scene at all; you don't jump back in time and then jump back to the present. To be really effective the two merge; there is no deliberate halt. That is why a few short flashbacks are often more effective than several long ones from which the reader has to be dragged back to the main body of the story. These short flashbacks should link past and present smoothly.

Even so, beware of using too many or they may appear as jagged interruptions. Used sparingly and well, they will merge into the story effortlessly.

Now, of course, you are recalling published novels which have depended largely on lengthy flashbacks, and others which have begun in the present and then continued retrospectively throughout the book, returning to the present only at the end. And you are justified in doing so. Skilled authors have produced successful novels that way, but I don't recommend that beginners should try to until they have some experience behind them. Whole chapters in flashback can lead to confusion until you have mastered the technique of getting back on to the main road again without any hitches or hiccups.

One last word on this retrospective device – write in the pluperfect tense as little as possible. This is sometimes called 'the had-had syndrome'. Example: he had had, she had had, they had had. To read consistently in the pluperfect can be jerky and irritating so, to avoid that, merely start the retrospective piece in the pluperfect if necessary, then merge into the present or normal tense until the end.

Clichés

Just as the use of too many adverbs, adjectives and dialogue tags betray an inexperienced author, so does the cliché betray the lazy one. To describe a young woman as 'a typical English Rose' – which, besides being a cliché, suggests that she is a natural blonde of gentle colouring and matching personality – can be misleading if she happens to be a brassily peroxided one who 'knows her way around'. Equally remiss is the masculine label of 'a typical sporting type' when sportsmen vary in appearance as vastly as do today's wide range of sports.

As for clichéd similes like 'proud as a peacock', 'mad as a March hare' or 'poor as a church mouse' – or any other hackneyed phrase – these also indicate that the writer can't be bothered to think of anything more original or more apt.

The lazy writer will also resort to clichéd openings like, 'Sunrise heralded the day as larks soared into the sky and the wind danced in the trees, while high upon a distant hill lambs frisked. . .', often with added description of the weather because it fills up the page or because the writer won't spare the time to exercise his imagination.

The cliché is a dangerous short cut, a device which enables you to toss off a piece of writing with a minimum of thought. But, being mortal, we are all in danger of falling into its trap. Nothing is so insidious as the cliché and nothing so effectively destroys good prose, so when you have finished a piece of work and are checking your final draft, wage war on it.

Endings

In many ways the winding up of your story is more difficult than the beginning, even though you may see it clearly ahead of you. At the start you have the whole vast canvas spread before you, yours to fill in any way you wish; at the end it has shrunk to a minimum and you are faced with the final test. In this limited space you must present the finale which readers are going to remember – with enjoyment, if it is satisfying, or with disappointment if it is not. On it can hinge their choice of whether or not to read your next book.

Think of that, and you won't toss off a slap-dash finish just because you want to be rid of the whole thing and to put your feet up at last. Don't imagine that because three quarters or more of the book has been exciting and well written, a swift curtain at the end is all that is needed, or that as long as everything is rounded off, readers can have no cause for disappointment.

But they can, and they will, and so will you when a publisher's reader describes the book as a let-down and doesn't recommend its publication; or, if it does get into print, word spreads that it fizzles out at the end, so copies remain on booksellers' shelves. After months of hard work, that situation can be a bitter one, so it is up to you to avoid it.

You can do this by giving the end as much thought as you gave to the beginning. Plan to leave your readers with a feeling of satisfaction and enjoyment on a par with the anticipation and excitement you engendered at the start.

Whatever the pessimists might say, I believe that readers prefer a happy ending to a miserable or depressing one. That doesn't mean they don't want anything 'true to life'; it means that even the saddest of stories can at least finish on a note of hope. Not everyone 'enjoys a good cry'; certainly not the readers of popular novels whether they be mystery, suspense, historical, or romance. As for crime novels, what the reader wants and expects and fully deserves to get is a surprising and convincing solution.

In short, the best ending is the one that totally satisfies. To achieve this, take good care not to let the action flag. Speed up the pace toward the end, but on a note of sustained excitement (similar to, but more final than, the chapter hook). And don't let the tale drag on for a dozen or so pages after the climax has been reached. Wind up the whole thing speedily, then leave your readers at the peak, reluctant to come down to earth. Such an ending will leave them asking when your next book is coming out.

10. Beating the Block

Recognising the causes

I often wish the term 'writer's block' had never been thought of because it seems to plant a conviction, in the minds of beginners, that the condition is part and parcel of authorship, even that one cannot *be* an author without suffering the dread disease. This is as misleading as advertising propaganda designed to convince people that they need some new product to cure ailments they never knew they had.

That all writers get stuck at times is well known, but anything that exaggerates a condition to the point of creating alarm is undesirable. The sudden inability to put words on paper is every author's bogey, but to give it such a heavy-handed name as 'writer's block' makes it sound immovable.

It isn't.

Early in Chapter 1, I mentioned two ways of dealing with two aspects of the problem; fear of starting ('starter's block') and the fear of being unable to follow up success ('the follow-up block'). I will now discuss others, with equally practical ways of coping.

The first step is to analyse what 'writer's block' is. George Eliot aptly summed it up as 'the pitiable instance of long incubation producing no chick'. There was no specific name for it in her day, but temporarily drying up was as familiar to authors then as it is now. Thomas Carlyle advised his poor wife, Jane, to abandon writing when the muse deserted her (as it frequently did after he became her husband), assuring her that 'eventually' the words would flow again, but this was suspect advice from a man who plainly did not want her to write at all, but only to be the dutiful wife catering for his needs and protecting him against disturbance – even to the extent of sending her to request neighbours to keep their cackling hens silent while he was writing.

So let's dismiss Thomas Carlyle, even though we cannot dismiss the block problem which can sometimes convince an author that he has written himself out, but such a case is unusual and to anticipate it is pessimistic. There are ways in which to confront and reverse the problem, so that you will eventually say, 'I never suffer from writer's block'. No one will believe you, but that won't worry you because you will be happily writing again.

Fear is invariably the main root of the problem. Fear can be mentally paralyzing and, as long as you let it take over, the dreaded block will master you instead of *you* mastering *it*.

The first step is not only to acknowledge your fear, but to diagnose the cause. There are numerous self-help books by experts on the subject, all of which, like medical dictionaries, will bog you down with sometimes incomprehensible terms and a wealth of symptoms which will convince you that you suffer from the lot. I propose to discard these experts along with Thomas Carlyle.

My only qualification is that I have survived every occupational hazard, including writer's block, and in the process have identified the different types and the various causes. Let's take them one by one.

The outline block

This can be suffered by those who are convinced that a writer *must* produce an outline because without it he won't know where he is going. Having already touched on that, it is unnecessary for me to dwell on it further, except to add that if you *are* working on an outline and have reached a point where a carefully planned scene breaks down, leaving you convinced that all that talk about characters 'taking over' and a story 'taking off on its own' is untrue, there can be a very simple reason for this apparent disaster, and one which many a writer has shared. You may have chosen the wrong background for your main character or characters, either social or physical; so see if you can switch it to another setting in which the behaviour you anticipated will be more natural.

Or, if you are writing an historical, check whether the time and place in which you have set your story (say seventeenth century London) has been researched thoroughly. It is important to remember that the London in your story would be vastly different from today, not only geographically, but culturally too. Check whether your blue print takes these changes fully into account, including changes in outlook and attitudes as well as in fashion, customs, and life styles. It is useless to expect your characters to react to specific situations in a specific way if the situations are inappropriate to their generation or time. They will metaphorically thumb their noses at you and your carefully mapped plan will fall apart.

When that happens, you feel a failure, but you are not. Bear in mind that a block is simply a red flag of warning, a signal that you are on the wrong lines. It is giving you a chance to rethink and rewrite.

Appropriately, I touched on 'starter's block' in Chapter 1, also on the 'follow-up block' which sometimes comes in the wake of sudden success, so the ways of dealing with them need not be reiterated. We can now go on to the ambition block.

The ambition block

Again, the name is my own for a condition which afflicts many aspiring authors, also many who have already achieved publication but feel dissatisfied without really knowing why. Unhappily, it can put a brake on a writer's career if he or she allows it to.

It is attributable to being too self-demanding, to setting your expectations too high, and to striving to emulate big literary names at whose shrines you have long worshipped. You read them with admiration and respect because they win awards and the highbrow literary journals praise them – and that, you believe, is the only *real* success. You therefore aspire to the same heights, become frustrated, and dry up.

You have come up against the 'ambition block' head on, and it is experienced by many who won't admit that they used to read less scholarly writings with enjoyment, but naturally put away such childish things when they set out to become serious (i.e. highbrow) writers. Not only would they not dream of reading at that level any more, they wouldn't dream of writing down to it. It would be demeaning. So they struggle and flounder and finish up in the most dangerous state of all, totally blocked and convinced they will never succeed.

If you are one of these people, take stock of yourself. Force yourself to be honest – and don't write another word until you have spent six months reading those authors whom you think you should despise because they *sell*. You won't enjoy all of them, you may not even finish some, but make a note of those which leave you with a feeling of satisfaction and enjoyment and then acknowledge that you have been reading at a level in which you feel at home. Then confess why. Confess that they struck a sympathetic chord, reflecting your own need to write the same type of fiction with the same spontaneity and the same lack of self-consciousness.

In this way you discover your natural bent. Recognising your limitations, *and being comfortable within them*, you will return to your pen or keyboard with this particular block effectively vanquished. And you won't be a bad writer because you have been sensible enough to come to terms with the truth.

The vanity block

You can cure this easily if you want to. It comes from trying to adhere to a picture of 'how an author should work' and even of 'how an author should look' (i.e. dripping with mink, if female; driving the latest Mercedes, if male). The picture becomes lodged in your mind; you can *see* yourself in the role, and to achieve it you know you must emulate the working methods of those who have already achieved it.

You have read how one particularly successful author writes from nine to five daily, with half an hour's break for lunch; or another who works every morning, relaxes in the afternoon playing golf, and returns to another long creative stint from eight to midnight. So *that's* how its done, you think (very impressed) and if you do the same you too will succeed. So your household and your family become geared to the chosen routine and then down comes the block. You are unproductive, worried, depressed, familiar once more with a sense of failure.

Here you must be honest again. Face up to the fact that *you* are not *that* person. You are someone else; different, individual. In the silence inflicted by this particular block your ego is urging you not only to think again, but to adapt to the circumstances of your life and to follow your personal inclinations. It will cease to protest once you abandon the idea that you must follow someone else's pattern.

The criticism block

This is perhaps the hardest to beat. I first experienced it at the age of thirteen and I remember it well. I read aloud a story I had written, of which I was secretly proud. I therefore expected my family to be proud too. Instead, one sister called it daft, another soppy, and the third was hard pressed to smother her laughter. I fled in tears. Never again would I write. Never, *ever*.

A day or two later my English teacher asked why I had not submitted a class essay. When she heard the reason she was not unsympathetic, but warned that until I learned to accept criticism I would fail at whatever I undertook. She then gave me a week to produce my essay and added another piece of advice. 'Remember that those who mock are usually those who can't do what *you* can.'

This truth has helped me to survive, but it is hard to cling to when comments are scathing. Writers have to live with this sensitivity and try to hide it. The hurts will linger, but you have to expurgate them. If you don't, they will block creativity more effectively than any other cause.

One way to counter adverse criticism, if you are unable to accept it silently, is a brief and pertinent *riposte* (if you have the opportunity and can think of it quicky enough!). There is a story about a popular romantic novelist of the thirties, Ruby M. Ayres, a large and genial lady who was apparently a match for anyone. In a fashionable London bar one day a patronising woman drawled, 'My dear, I could *never* read books like yours!'

'Maybe not,' boomed Ruby, 'but could you write 'em?'

Once you are published, a good way to endure criticism is to look at your royalty figures. They can exhilerate you more than any praise because they would not be there if denigration of your work was universal.

If you are determined to become a published author, you are sure to devise your own ways of beating the block, whatever its cause. I used to suffer difficulty in re-launching after a prolonged break. I now resolutely leave a scene unfinished when (but only when) I can see precisely where it is going. Leaving reminder notes on my word processor, I can then return to my desk quite ready to continue; no permanent break, no block.

Another method, and one I recommend for getting into the flow again, is to go back a few pages and start editing. Rewriting or reshaping bad patches creates a launching pad and words then continue to flow when the next sheet of paper is a blank one.

Both are simple remedies, but don't forget that, whenever you get stuck, the first step is to root out the cause of the problem.

11. Sagas, Sequels, and Settings

The continuing tale

Every writer of fiction feels possessive toward his or her characters, but even stronger is the feeling of being possessed *by* them. Sometimes this lingers after a novel is finished, as if they were hammering on the door, demanding readmission. Even so, I was surprised when the Drayton family 'took me over'. At the end of the first volume, *The Drayton Legacy*, I fully expected to say goodbye to them and to open my mind to others. I might have achieved this had the Draytons allowed me to, but they did not, and when the publishers suggested I should write a sequel I found, after initial resistance, that I wanted to, if only to get that eighteenth century family of potters out of my mind.

Once acknowledging the truth, I also acknowledged that part of my reluctance had been due to cowardice. I had never tackled a sequel and had heard, from some who had, that it was a difficult process and one to be resolutely avoided. To me, that was a challenge, as a result of which I learned that writing a sequel is not the terrifying experience I expected. Evidence of this was supported by the many family sagas on library shelves and the number of authors who had woven entirely new stories about various branches of a family. Thus I realised that my sequel had to be a novel capable of standing on its own. Even though growing out of what had gone before, it had to be a separate and self-contained book which could, if necessary, be read out of sequence although retaining links with its forerunner.

Ironically, the final decision to tackle it was spurred by a sequel written by an author who went about the task in what I consider to be entirely the wrong way. I read it with a combination of astonishment and not a little annoyance. I had not bought Book 2 expecting to find repetitive material from Book 1, but in the belief that the second book would be as new to me as the first. Instead, almost the first quarter of the sequel was

113

re-hashed material from its predecessor, some pages even being reprinted verbatim, with slices of new material injected here and there. Not until page 217 did this unsatisfactory sequel really begin to cover fresh fields.

I am not denying that it is necessary to acquaint new readers with essential facts from the past, but it should be done in a wholly new way so that the readers of the first book find it acceptable.

There were other object lessons in this cut-the-corner author's sequel and I took care to avoid them in Drayton 2 (*The Potter's Niece*), making sure it should not only contain *no* reprinted material, even in patches, but that slabs of retrospection should not be inserted just to put new readers in the picture (or to pad out the story); that the earlier part of Book 2 should not be a virtually condensed synopsis of what had gone before because people who had read Book 1 would be likely to remember a great deal and feel defrauded (as I did) if it were fed to them again; and, finally and most important, that unless I could come up with a totally new novel I should not attempt a sequel at all.

The Drayton Legacy was never intended to be the first of a series. It had been written as a single, complete book and a single, complete book it was; all problems solved; all questions answered; all loose ends tidied off. So what threads were left for me to pick up and weave into a sequel? That is the question you must ask yourself if you consider writing a sequel. My own answer was – none.

It was the characters, not the situations on which the curtain had fallen, that cried out to live again. Naturally, some of the family had died or, no longer useful to the story, had been phased out, but I could see how their deeds and misdeeds forecast the future. Such shadows, through their influence on events, would become a natural part of the sequel and take the story forward again. So, too, would Drayton descendants, some of whom had already been born.

So back I had to go to the family, whose ancestors had been itinerant potters since the fifteenth century, digging their clay wherever they could find it and peddling their wares throughout the highways and byways of England until one enterprising Drayton set up the first family pottery in an abandoned barn. To convey such information at length in Book 2 for the benefit of new readers, or even to introduce it retrospectively, would put a brake on action; but to filter it in unobtrusively through occasional references to the past, recalled nostalgically by older members of the family, or talking about the family heritage to a young grandson, would add necessary colour and interest as well as sow seeds for future events.

Thus I learned the value of sifting one's existing material carefully and deciding which events in the first book would inevitably lead to new events in the second, bonding the past with the present.

Seeking an opening from the past

An effective start to the sequel did not appear to be a major problem until I turned to the end of *The Drayton Legacy*. It had closed with the murder of the tyrannical Joseph whose wife, Agatha, pretended to mourn him while his sister, Phoebe, openly wept for him. Phoebe had idolized her brother and held him up as an example to her errant husband. From the beginning there had been rivalry between the two women, and at the close of Book 1 Phoebe had triumphed over her sister-in-law by being the first to become pregnant, inwardly gloating because Agatha, now widowed, would never be. It meant that Phoebe's child would inherit vast estates over which she, Phoebe, could reign until the child came of age.

Plainly, there had to be an unexpected start to the sequel and this presented itself in answer to the ever-useful *what if?* What if Agatha had discovered, soon after her husband's death, that she too was pregnant, and what if she had later given birth to a son, the direct male heir who would supercede Phoebe's child, a daughter? Such a position could present further possibilities, with scheming Phoebe planning a possible marriage between the two – since marriage between first cousins was not against Church of England law.

But when to take the curtain up? If I did that at the time of the boy's birth, the story threatened to meander through his uneventful childhood. A leap ahead was desirable, so the opening I chose was his coming-of-age celebrations, at which his behaviour demonstrated that he was indeed his father's son and enabled elderly relatives to recall brief flashbacks into the past. These were planted to whet the interest of new readers and to serve as bridges, linking past and present, in order to satisfy former ones.

In short, I had to keep in mind both those who had read the first book and those who had not. Both had to be catered for and I soon realised that satisfying one while satisfying the other was perhaps the trickiest part of all. I also realised that when writing a sequel or a trilogy (into which I developed the story of the Drayton family), the author has to look continuously toward the future while continuously being aware of the past. Tentacles from the past must only be used to propel the sequel forward or to shed light on a current situation.

Conversation is a useful way in which to present essential facts about the past – through one character telling another, or through two or three characters exchanging reminiscences, or even through the desire of one person to clarify or atone for past misunderstandings – but always and *only* if such reminiscence or clarification is needed to advance the new story. And always briefly. Brevity can not only have a greater impact, it can forestall hold-ups. A sequel must travel forward at the same pace as its predecessor, with the same independence of structure and plot.

Bearing these lessons in mind, you will find that, once launched into your sequel, it will proceed at the same tempo and with the same amount of effort required for any novel, and is therefore no easier nor more difficult to write. And if you put your heart into it, it will be as alive to your readers as the first book so that, at the end, they are wanting yet another to follow, and when you are faced with that, you will be faced with the all-important matter of updating the background.

Nothing in life remains static, which means that backgrounds, and the people you set down in them, will change from period to period. Between the action in Books 1 and 2 of my saga was a gap of twenty-one years; between Books 2 and 3, a further fifteen. In those time gaps not only fashions had changed, but also industrial methods and, to a certain degree (but not so greatly as in a modern story) lifestyles and attitudes, all of which had an influence on situations, developments and characters. Inevitably, this meant further research.

Getting the background right

There seems to be a widely held belief, among new writers, that background is simply the geographical setting of a story, but it is a great deal more than that. It is not only the place where your characters live and work, but how they live and the work they do; it is their cultural level and the strata of society to which they belong; it is customs, habits, traditions, language, food, dress, beliefs and attitudes. It can be city or country life, moral or immoral, ethnic or non-ethnic, industrial or leisured, rich or poor. Above all, background is made up of the essential details that give authenticity to your story, whatever its time and setting.

The suggestions I give for getting your background right are the result of experience over many years. Don't be deterred because I sometimes issue them as warnings. 'How not to' can often be more constructive than 'how to'; 'don't' more effective than 'do'.

Don't fake background details. Don't imagine that readers won't be knowledgeable enough to catch you out, or that if you choose an unusual subject and try to 'blind them with science' a few fabrications will pass unnoticed. The fact that your subject happens to be unusual will be no guarantee that amongst the mass of readers there won't be one, and possibly more, who will actually be well versed in it and will spot at least one mistake – and one is one too many.

No author can afford to lose credibility. If your main character breeds huskies in Alaska or rare Chinese pheasants in Kiang-si, don't think you can get away with imagining the creature's eating habits or any other detail about their rearing. Learn everything there is to learn about rearing huskies or Chinese pheasants, or you can be assured that someone, somewhere, will know and will enjoy putting you right.

The easiest way to safeguard against errors is, of course, to write only about things you know, but sometimes that can be restrictive and, if you have a fertile and questing imagination, it will be carrying you into realms that need exploring. That is where research comes in.

Research

When I began writing this book I made up my mind that I would *not* quote the much-used cliché about the iceberg – that only the tip shows, but beneath lies the unseen mass without which it would sink – yet now that I need an example of the amount of research necessary to add authenticity to a background, I can think of none better. Only a small amount of your researched material may, and probably will, be needed to give conviction to your story, but that small amount must be supported by a depth of knowledge. When an author writes with authority, it shows. When he merely slots in scraps of information picked up here and there, it also shows. And when that happens credibility flies out of the window.

Perhaps you have decided to set your story in Singapore or some other distant place. It would help enormously if you could spend some time there, but if this is impossible you do the next best thing; you read about the place, browse through travel brochures, hire video films and dream up your own imaginary picture with the result that what you eventually write reads like a travelogue. That is *not* your aim and you vow never again to write about places you don't actually know. Is this the right decision? No.

Many highly successful books have been set in countries physically unknown to their authors, but the research which produced them has been extensive and intensive. It has gone 'way beyond the travel brochure stage. It has delved into the country's history; it has studied the inhabitants' way of life, their culture, architecture, educational system, religion, traditions, and every other possible aspect. All this, and more, has provided that great mass of material which gave strength and authenticity to the essential amount threaded into the story, lifting it above superficiality.

If, however, your story is set almost entirely in the industrial or manufacturing or any other specialised background, you will need less of the social scene outside it. The large stage of a university or factory or school or multiple store, or any similar establishment, can offer ample space for all that takes place, focusing on the personal competitiveness, the wheeling and dealing, the secret and not-so-secret personal relationships and animosities and emotional undercurrents. You can inter-relate the stories of a dozen or more characters in any highly concentrated background (read Arthur Hailey's *Hotel* or *Airport* as examples) but the need for accuracy is as great and every detail must count.

Penetrating research on this scale has produced many successful blockbusters but, take heart, there is no need to exhaust yourself in the process. You don't have to carry out *all* your research in one massive effort, unless you feel you would work

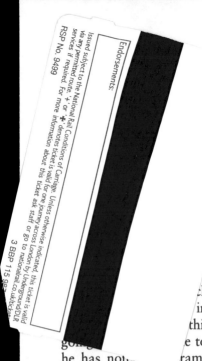

Research

do, but many hard working
y work as is needful to get
rite, halting when they come to
ng with additional information,
blems. The experience is rather
l block, forcing you to halt until
you have to clear it yourself.
ct as a stimulus, forcing you away
ble sessions in your local reference
kshops, including second-hand ones
ure-trove. You will certainly want and
n reference shelves at home, not only
satisfaction of having essential books
ch you enjoy browsing) ready to hand.
interviews with experts. A best-selling
this method for almost his entire research,
e top and at every strata downward until
he has not. rammed with information covering every
level of the enterprise, and then asking for more if necessary. It
is rarely, if ever, refused.

You will find that people love to talk about the sphere in
which they work, and especially about their own particular
participation in it, but you would be wise to consult more than
one because on some points even experts in most areas can
disagree. It will be up to you to assess their opinions and decide
which to accept. On debatable points, try to get written
confirmation of their statements so that you may quote them
should you be challenged. It would also be wise to ask the
experts for permission to do so. If they prefer not to be quoted,
you may have good reason to doubt their reliability. If they
agree without hesitation, you are on safer ground – but still try
to get it in writing.

What other sources will you consult, apart from major
libraries? There are public record offices, museums, local history
and church archives, private memoirs if you can gain access to
them, and countless other sources, all of which are listed in Ann
Hoffmann's *Research For Writers*. This valuable book should
be one of the first you buy for your personal reference library,
for it not only lists extensive research sources, but also gives
expert advice on research methods and on some of the pitfalls
to be avoided by the inexperienced writer.

Using your research effectively

When you have assembled your background material, don't feed it into your story in huge chunks. Spread it unobtrusively so that atmosphere is built up imperceptibly and naturally. Never stop your story dead in its tracks for long passages of description or information. Always remember that readers can't be conned. They recognise when an author is cramming in material just for the sake of doing so, and they will put their own interpretation on it – usually that he is trying to impress them with his knowledge or, if the background is an exotic one, trying to show that he is accustomed to luxury travel. Their assumptions are, of course, very wide of the truth, but how are they to know that the author just can't bear to waste his precious research?

All the same, economy must be the keynote. Too much elaboration can burden a story, so don't overpaint the picture. I recently read a novel set in Burma, crammed with repetitive Burmese names and forms of address, lumbered with too much Burmese history and littered with incomprehensible Burmese words and titles. A glossary was inserted at the end of the book to aid interpretation, but continual recourse to it meant breaks in concentration so that eventually one ceased to bother. It was the author's first novel so one made allowances – but not for the publisher, who should have known better.

Integrate your background facts with the action and the story will be a hundred times more real. Interweave such paragraphs with the execution of the plot, and your readers will not only be carried along with it, but absorb its atmosphere.

'But what of all that wasted research?' you may ask. 'What of all the precious material I didn't use? What am I supposed to do, throw it away?'

Indeed, no. Save it. You have a precious stock for future books; the mere fact that you have such a store will inspire you to write another. For years I hoarded information about Victorian womanhood from the time dear Mama launched her daughters on to the marriage market to the time they became wives and mothers. Social, marital, sexual, child care, domestic, fashion, transport, etiquette; every possible aspect of a woman's life whatever her standing, from the lowly coachman's wife in the mews to the high society hostess; from the sweat-shop seamstress to the middle and upper class housewife; from the 'fallen woman' to the society courtesan; from the kitchen maid to the housekeeper; from the country miss who never set foot in London to the débutante's presentation at Buckingham Palace. I amassed so much that even after four Victorian novels I had used scarcely half of it. Eventually I collected it all together and turned it into a comprehensive reference book, *The Model Wife, Nineteenth Century Style*. So never part with researched material. You never know what you can do with it.

The period novel v the historical

It is not the intention of this book to concentrate on the writing of one particular genre; indeed, it is impossible since the term 'popular fiction' covers such a vast range. But while we are on the subject of research it seems apt to discuss one genre which can demand more research than almost any other, with the possible exception of a modern blockbuster concentrating on the complexities of a vast technological background. The genre I am referring to now is the historical and its close rival, the period novel.

Some people argue that they are one and the same thing, but to me they are not. The dividing line may be thin, but it is there, and to define it should be of some help.

The background to a genuine historical novel relies on recorded historical events and, in particular, on people associated with them; people who actually lived and whose names have passed into posterity – such as the first Queen Elizabeth, Mary Queen of Scots, Henry the Eighth and his six wives, and other names passed down through the centuries, either because of their birth, their achievements, their scandals, or because they just happened to be around when some memorable event occurred, which involved them.

In contrast, for plot and characterization the period novel relies almost entirely on the author's imagination. This is not to say that the background can be inaccurate. Far from it. As much research must go into the period novel as into the true historical. Authenticity of fashions, food, housing, transport, domesticity, speech, education (or lack of it), etiquette, manners and morals, social strata, family life, plus political background of the time – all must be researched and accurately presented in both types of fiction.

For example, let's take the period novel. Even if politics and notable politicians of the past don't play an active or influential part in it, passing references to the reigning prime minister, or to the fact that a specific battle, such as the Crimean or the American War of Independence, is raging overseas, add authority and colour to the background and help to pinpoint the exact period, but that can be the extent of their usefulness if the author so wishes.

Examples of true period novels are Georgette Heyer's Regency and Georgian romances, as opposed to her historical novels such as *The Infamous Army, Royal Escape,* and *The Conqueror.* It is for her imaginative and sparkling period pieces that she is most remembered and which won her acclaim.

Plainly, she loved the Regency and Georgian periods above all, her ear so attuned to speech modes of the time that she could create pseudo phrases and slang expressions which sounded as authentic as those that were. Her readers accepted these imaginary colloquialisms as genuine examples of Georgian and Regency speech. Many are untraceable through the usual idiomatic research channels, but it is easy to imagine that had Regency bucks and Georgian belles heard them, they would have adopted them eagerly.

The important thing was that she captured the insouciance of their period and the flippancy of their verbal exchanges, and that she maintained this skill until, with *My Lord John,* she strayed into medieval history, which she researched with diligence but marred with the use of dialogue spiced with unmistakeable modern slang and doubtful medieval phrases on which sharp-eyed critics pounced. In contrast, the true historical, by such writers as Margaret Irwin for example, would have been researched beyond military or political events of the time; dialectal and idiomatic speech would have been delved into with equal thoroughness and presented accurately.

But when it came to the period novel, Georgette Heyer could never be faulted on any background point. When she said that a stage-coach left The George in Southwark at specific intervals and at specific times, any witch hunter seeking to catch her out would fail. Stage-coach timetables of the period proved her right time and time again.

It is logical that if you are obsessed with a once-living character in recorded history, the urge to use them as a central figure will be irresistible, and because you will wish to achieve an accurate portrayal of them, you will research deeply into their biographical details because someone, somewhere, may well challenge you about them – besides which, you will want your portrayal to be as true as you can make it. For the period novel, on the other hand, since you *create* many of the characters you can also create their personalities. This gives the writer of the period novel a big advantage over the writer of the historical.

The genuine historical novel demands adherence to documented facts. It governs, whereas the period novel indulges, but at the same time it is not totally restrictive. It can take a slice of recorded history and present it either conventionally or with question and provocation. It can challenge and even take certain liberties providing it works within the framework of recorded facts.

This is not to say that a chosen time cannot shackle the 'period' author to some extent, making it difficult and even impossible to change to another. In that event it is useless to try to switch the story to the Georgian, Victorian, Plantagenet, Tudor, Elizabethan or any other period as the case may be. If it needs background atmosphere relevant only to a particular time, your setting and characters must naturally arise from it; beyond that, the story is wholly yours.

A classic example of a period novel is *The Mill on the Floss,* a wholly imaginative story dealing with ordinary folk of the day, but which could have been equally successful set in another early period. In contrast, for a classic example of an historical novel wholly dependent on well authenticated historical events we need look no further than *A Tale of Two Cities.*

Using exotic backgrounds

For a certain type of light romantic fiction a glamorous geographical background may well have advantages over a mundane one, but outside such a category this now appears to be doubtful. Today, the domestic scene at many levels seems to be holding its own.

But if you really want to use an exotic background, don't be discouraged by those who warn you that a particular setting has been 'done to death'. It is true that the *Raj Quartet* and *Far Pavilions* preceded a spate of novels set in India, but the background was not 'done to death' as a result. That happened only to poor imitations. Similarly, Hong Kong has inspired countless novels; so many that the pessimistic warning should have discouraged James Clavell from producing *Noble House*. The success of that novel should demonstrate that if you have a strong feeling for a particular background and passionately want to use it you may certainly do so, but explore it thoroughly first. If you cannot visit it (and even if you can) read everything on which you can lay your hands.

First you must study the history of the place; read the most comprehensive and authenticated volume you can find, from cover to cover. This will serve you better than several brief or sketchy ones and, when you start to write, keep it beside you for reference. This will prevent you from making mistakes on dates, times, and other historical facts you may use. Also read memoirs and biographies of people who have left their mark on the place or contributed to its history. You may use little or perhaps none of it in your story, but through your awareness of it you will get a greater 'feel' of the place and a sense of identification which will increase as you accumulate the further mass of detail necessary to bring your background to life.

Sociological studies are invaluable and, for other essential facts, travel brochures and travel books can yield useful information on food, shopping, customs, traditions, religious ceremonies and festivals, table and social manners, medical practices, levels of society, immigrant or refugee population, currency, sports, train routes, bus routes, taxi fares, markets, and agricultural and horticultural specialities of the region. No facts can be too small or too unimportant to harvest.

You will be wise to get a large and up-to-date wall map of the region if you are writing in the present day (and by hook or by crook one of the period in which you are writing if the story is set in earlier times). You will also need the latest road maps and street maps and copies of the prevailing motoring laws. Travel brochures will supply you with names and locations of popular stores and restaurants. The Press Offices of appropriate consulates and legations can also prove helpful.

You will also be wise to get some basic grounding in the language of the country to enable you to use correctly spoken sentences when needed – and when you have written your dialogue, do get an authoritative checking. Representative consulates or trade centres based in this country have been known to prove helpful by providing contacts, and language schools are always worth approaching.

More novels with foreign settings are written by people who have never been there than readers would suspect, but it is done the hard way. But nowhere in this book do I say that authorship is easy.

How much of your research to filter into your work is something you will learn instinctively the more you write. If, when reading through the finished story, you sense that you have put in too much, be brave. Cut it out and save it for another book. You won't regret it.

Highlighting a scene

Geographical backgrounds, and particularly specific locations, can be used successfully to sharpen an individual scene. By focusing on a well known landmark your reader will see it vividly and the scene will have greater impact. If, for instance, you have chosen London for your setting and you have a dramatic situation – say a showdown between two characters – you can make it more effective by setting it on or by some famous spot, such as Westminster Bridge with the Houses of Parliament towering behind and Big Ben booming the hour while homeward-going crowds push unseeingly by, or cast fleeting glances of curiosity or amusement. The picture will be visually stronger whether the reader is familiar with London or not, because such landmarks are world famous.

For comparison, set the scene in an ordinary room in an ordinary house in an ordinary street. . . and see how much more vivid is the first. At such moments, background is your ally. Make the most of it.

A final warning

Before leaving the subject of research, one cautionary note. The fascination of the task can become addictive. The sense of discovery, and the excitement of learning the hitherto unknown, can become mesmeric, enticing you on until you can forget what you were looking for initially and be sidetracked into pastures new. There are writers, of whom I am admittedly one, who enjoy research so much that they are easily led astray. So don't be tempted. Be resolute. Remember the job in hand and get on with it.

12. Getting into Print

Preparing your manuscript

Now to the vital problem of marketing your work. The question of manuscript presentation may seem unimportant to beginners, but it is the first impression an editor receives of you, and first impressions count. A slip-shod, untidy manuscript, full of spelling errors, bad punctuation and grammar, is enough to discourage any overworked editor from reading it. Least welcome of all is the hand-written submission.

Although the word 'manuscript' literally means something written by hand, the word is widely used when referring to an author's typescript. This is the professional approach, so never submit hand-written work. No publisher will accept it as final copy. Could inexperienced authors see some manuscripts that arrive in the 'slush pile' – the term by which unsolicited work, as opposed to commissioned, is unkindly (though not always inaptly) known – they would understand why. Most handwritten manuscripts are difficult to read, many almost illegible and, when dog-eared, bear silent witness to successive rejections.

Even if clean and reasonably neat, can you blame publishers' readers for turning to typescripts which can be read more easily and more quickly, and can therefore expedite a decision?

Today the competition is fierce, so it is worth submitting your work as professionally presented as possible. If you don't possess a typewriter, either invest in one or, if you can afford it, a word processor because of its many advantages. Since supply and demand have brought prices down, many many reasonable package deals are available, and bear in mind that self-employment enables you to set office equipment against tax, also professional fees if you use a secretarial service.

Presentation and layout

Type your story in double spacing on good quality A4 paper, never on flimsy or very thick, and on one side of the sheet only. If you are uncertain, go to a really good office stationer and ask to see samples of paper suitable for authors' manuscripts. It can range from 60 to 80 gsm in weight. 60 gsm is too light, 70 passable, but 75 to 80 is best. I always used 75 gsm until I found a satisfactory 80 gsm which looks and feels like 75 but with additional strength, of a good whiteness, and at a very fair price. Buying a dozen or more reams at a time (500 sheets per ream) is economical.

The old foolscap and quarto sizes have been eclipsed by A4. I have heard it said that quarto should still be used for submission to America, but have never found this to be so.

If you work on a typewriter, use a plain black ribbon and one that is not splodgy. A clear typeface can be maintained by cleaning the keys, or daisy wheel, with a short-bristled brush dipped lightly in methylated spirit, or one of those type-cleaning sheets of stiffened paper with a magnetic surface which cleans the letters as you type any of the legendary test lines incorporating every letter and digit on the keyboard. Expensive sprays are also available, but for a thorough job the thick, stumpy, well-bristled typing brush is best. A new toothbrush will do providing it is strong, and the common pin cannot be beaten for dealing with letters in which dirt can lodge, such as 'a', 'b', 'm' and others with small cavities.

All pages must be numbered in sequence. With a word processor, this is done automatically in a Header or Footer (at the head or foot of the page). It is also a good idea to include the title of the work and the author's name on the same line. Should one page be accidentally mislaid (easily done when reading a lengthy typescript at an overladen editorial desk), re-identifying and re-slotting it will be easier and less time wasting. Adding the author's name also helps – like this:

Nora Ralldan   *Writing to Sell – p.23 –*

The whole line can be centred, or split between left and right of the page, as above.

Equipping yourself for the job

I know several established writers who regard their 'good old bangers' as longtime friends and shun anything more sophisticated, but the speed at which word processors have developed, and are still developing, has established them as virtual necessities and certainly the most popular equipment for authors.

Another thing in their favour is that many book publishers now ask commissioned authors to submit work on disk. This certainly saves the author printing-off time and postage costs, though care should be taken to keep back-up copies. They are as important to a writer as carbon copies used to be.

Another piece of equipment worth investing in is a good photocopier. Some writers might deem it unnecessary, but its uses are manifold and, like any piece of time-saving equipment, a godsend in a busy author's life. As with word processors, reasonably priced and reasonably sized photocopiers can also be found, but avoid the very small 'desktop' models if you want long life and reliable performance. If money is limited it is worth searching for a good restorer of second hand models. Tell him exactly what you require in size and weight and performance and if he cannot supply it immediately, ask him to look out for one while you do likewise. The thought of competition could spur him into action.

Since supply and demand have brought prices down in practically all ranges of computerized office equipment, many reasonable deals are available. It is also useful to know that self-employment (if you become a full-time author) entitles you to certain tax advantages, details of which can be obtained from your local taxation office.

But why bother with a photocopier if you have disks and need only run another print-off if needed? It's a matter of choice. Personally, I like to read from printed pages rather than switching on a word processor and reading from a screen at which I have already been staring for long, and sometimes tiring, spells. Another advantage is that a good photocopier can produce print-perfect manuscripts should you be asked to provide another, as well as business documents and items of all kinds necessary to your work, without losing valuable time in visiting your nearest copying centre.

Why is good presentation so important?

Because a clean and clear manuscript saves a lot of time when preparing it for publication. It is not only the copy editor who appreciates this, it is everyone involved.

The copy editor is the person who 'sees the book to bed'. Many women succeed in this responsible job, which demands much more work than is imagined by the uninitiated. Checking grammar and punctuation is the very least of her responsibilities. Author's facts also have to be checked, inconsistencies and repetitions removed, and suggestions made for re-phrasing badly constructed or ambiguously worded sentences. The script must be combed for inaccuracies, doubtful issues queried, and suggestions put forward for reshuffling passages if such transitions would improve the book or speed up action or eliminate dragging patches.

When your script comes back for approval before going to press (always sought by a good copy editor because the book is your creation and your copyright) you may recoil from what appears to be carnage, but after taking a good look you will usually see sense behind it. Every author should be thankful for a good copy editor. If you are unlucky enough to get a bad one, you can only pray that his or her editorial days will be numbered.

You can now see why a good typescript is appreciated by everyone, how much valuable time it can save, and why your co-operation is worthwhile.

Page set-up

Margins of approximately 1.50 inches at each side, as well as at the head and foot of the page, are important, not only making your script easier to read but also enabling the copy editor to insert instructions to the printer. Allocate a fixed number of double spaced lines per page, including one for the page number at the top or foot. If you are word processing, slot these into 'page set-up' and all will be taken care of automatically thereafter.

Page numbering

One of the assets of word processing is that consecutive numbering is done automatically and cannot get out of order or skip a page – though some models don't number the first page of a chapter on the principle that such pages are not numbered in published books, so they proceed to the next page, numbering correctly thereafter. If you dislike this practice, check that any word processor you are considering does not include it.

The title page

Always include a title (or 'front') page. On this, print your name and address in the top right hand corner, or your agent's should you be using one. Centre the story's title lower down with the author's name, also centred, a few spaces below. Nearer the foot of the page state what rights you are offering. Should you be submitting to a magazine, this line should indicate First British Serial Rights (1st BSR or, as some people put it, FBSR).

The sale of FBSR permits the magazine or newspaper to print the work once only, whether a short story or the serialisation of a novel prior to publication; after which the remaining serial rights, including foreign, remain with the author – though the book publisher may stipulate in his contract that his company takes a percentage of post-publication fees, such as for library or large print editions, or translation sales.

Certain clauses in book publishers' contracts are usually negotiable, so if you feel strongly on certain points, and have no agent to act for you, don't be afraid to ask for a discussion. Publishers, on the whole, are not ogres.

Publication rights are many and complex. Should you not have an agent to act for you and are a member of the Society of Authors, you can seek their advice regarding any proposed contract.

The question of length

It is helpful, though not essential, to indicate on the title page the approximate length, or wordage, of your book. If the work has been commissioned, an approximate length will have been agreed and will be confirmed in the contract, sometimes as 'between 70,000 and 80,000 words' or 'not more than 100,000 words'. When you reach the enviable heights of well established authorship, length is sometimes not stipulated at all. At that stage in your career both you and your publisher will silently agree that the book shall be as long or as short as the story demands, but if you wish to calculate the length without the help of a word count on your machine, the best method of doing so has been issued by publishers Robert Hale Limited. With their consent, I include it below.

The purpose of calculating the wordage of any typescript is to determine the number of printed pages it will occupy. The precise word count is of no use since it tells us nothing about the number of short lines resulting from paragraphing or dialogue (particularly important in fiction).

Calculation is therefore based on the assumption that all printed pages have no paragraph beginnings or endings and the type area is completely filled with words.

To assess the wordage proceed as follows:

1. Ensure the typewriting is the same throughout in the terms of size, length of line etc. If not, the procedure given below should be followed separately for each individual style of typing and the results added together.
2. Count 50 full-length lines and find the average number of words – e.g. 50 lines of 560 words gives an average of 11.2 words.
3. Average the number of lines over 10 characteristic pages – e.g. 245 lines on 10 pages gives an average of 24.5 lines.
4. Multiply the averages of 2 and 3 to get average per page – e.g. 11.2 x 24.5 = 274.
5. Ensure the page numbering is consecutive then multiply the word average per page by the number of pages (count short pages at beginnings and ends of chapters as full pages).
6. Draw attention to, but do not count, foreword, preface, introduction, bibliography, appendices, index, maps or other line figures.

Finally, repeat your name and address in the bottom right hand corner of the last page of typescript.

Despatching the manuscript

Paper clips can be used for short stories, but not for joining chapter pages of a book. They can trap other papers and prove an irritant. Pins can be even worse, as many a red spot on a page can testify. Staples are equally unpopular, necessitating removal by hand (usually with the fingernail.) If packing in a jiffy bag or something similar, secure the bundle of loose sheets with elastic bands. You can protect them with cardboard on top and beneath.

Bound typescripts can be cumbersome and, in any case, will have to be unbound for despatch to a printer. If you really want to bind the sheets, use a loose-ringed binder from which they can be extracted easily.

The best and most acceptable method is to send the loose pages packed in the supplier's box. My long-ago editorial experience taught me this, also the best way to read them. Placing the opened box on my desk, and the empty lid upturned beside it, I would then automatically replace each page face down in the lid until, reaching the end, I could upturn the whole thing and be back at the beginning. This is an infallible way to keep a manuscript in numerical order when reading.

The greatest service the word processor has performed for author and editor is destroying the need for carbon copies. If you have ever dealt with smudged and blurred scripts (especially those which have been on a long trail before reaching you) you will understand the discomfort of strained eyes and the abomination of blackened fingers. Mercifully, we are spared those 'primitive' methods now, for even public libraries and good stationers offer access to photocopying equipment at realistic prices per page. Charges at photocopying bureaux vary.

It is usual to send your top copy to the publisher and keep its photocopy for your files (unless, like Bantam Press, a publisher stipulates otherwise). It is often useful to keep two in case, on acceptance, you are asked to supply a duplicate. You may also be asked to supply one for the cover artist's use and some publishers even stipulate the supply of two manuscripts as a contractual clause.

If supplying disks instead of mss, make sure you have checked them for accuracy and that your back-up copies are identical.

The moral of all this is – penny-pinching on your presentation is false economy. Aim for a good standard, and maintain it.

G P – two initials to remember

I always maintain that these two letters are, to an author, the most important in the alphabet; and no, they don't stand for

General Practitioner but for Grammar and Punctuation. I mention them here because they feature largely when you finally check your completed script. At that stage you must watch for them, lynx-eyed. The same applies to spelling.

I once gave an evening talk to a local writers' circle. When it came to question time I was struck by the persistence of a woman at the back who raised her hand repeatedly despite the spate of questions which, due to an officious 'Madam Chairman' I was obliged to answer as she selected, but I was very aware of the persistent lady and determined she should be given a hearing. Plainly, she had something to ask which no one else had thought of.

To get an unusual question is both a joy and a challenge so eventually, and determinedly, I forestalled the officious 'Madam Chairman' and called on the patient lady.

Far from being worth waiting for, her question was a let-down.

'What do you do if you can't spell?'

When I suggested she should work with a dictionary beside her, she replied that it would take up too much time. She added that she 'would have thought it was the publisher's job to check all spelling anyway'. She also saw no reason why she should bother with grammar and punctuation because 'that should be the copy editor's job, not the author's'. Nor did she appreciate my argument that a person who is being paid to do a professional job should approach it with a professional attitude. As for checking and revising a manuscript until it was as near perfect as she could make it – plainly, she thought me a fusser.

She became more and more truculent until I finally asked how she would feel if a dressmaker delivered an unfinished garment to her, saying it would take up too much of her time to turn up the hem or take out the tackings or do any finishing off, so she would have to do all that for herself and still pay the bill. Only then did the questioner subside, very sulkily.

I am not saying that an author is expected to be a perfectionist; what I *am* saying is that it is a good idea to try. None of us is infallible. We all make mistakes. Some of us are good at spelling and others are not, and the same applies to our knowledge of English, but for this very reason any author worth their salt takes a pride in their work and in its presentation. If spelling is not your strong suit, follow my suggestion and work with a dictionary beside you; check doubtful words as you write, or make a note of them and check at the end of your day's writing stint so you won't forget about them. This method will also save considerable time when checking the complete manuscript before preparing it for submission.

The same applies to grammar and punctuation. I have already commented on the use of adverbs and adjectives, so a brief word now about the split infinitive – that tiresome variation of the infinitive verb which seems to be increasingly prevalent today.

Here is a simple example: 'She started to quickly run across the road.'

In our schooldays it was drummed into us that to split the infinitive (to insert a word or words between *to* and its verb) was a heinous crime, and good copy editors still frown on it. My own aversion is because it often makes a sentence sound awkward. The example should have read: 'She started to run quickly across the road,' which sounds fine, but on the other hand there is such a thing as the justified split infinitive. Of this, C E Metcalfe quotes an example: 'We regret it is impossible to legally authorise the termination of the lease.' Correctly written this should be: 'We regret it is impossible to authorise legally the termination of the lease.' But which reads more smoothly? In that instance the split would seem to be justified.

In the interests of a more melodious use of words, many people are willing to accept the hitherto unacceptable, but the safest thing is to avoid splitting the infinitive if you can. If you can't, then 'play safe' and remodel the sentence.

A jarring grammatical mistake, and one which is becoming more widely used in speech, in the press, in literature, and amongst the reputedly cultured, is the use of 'different to'. Arguments that it is permissible are unconvincing when countered with 'similar from', which is instantly recognised as contradictory and, like 'different to', wrong. To avoid any misuse, it is a good idea to repeat 'different *from*' and 'similar *to*' in one's mind until correct usage becomes automatic.

Similar errors to avoid are 'try and' for 'try to', 'loan' for 'lend' (*loan* is a noun and *lend* is a verb, but they are commonly confused – eg: 'she loaned me a book' instead of 'she lent me. . .'. Also the use of 'that' in conjunction with an adjective or instead of a simple 'so' . . . 'I was that happy' and 'I was that angry', or 'I don't think he's that clever' should be '. . .so happy', '. . .so angry', and '. . .so clever'. All such usages can jar when read, even though they pass unnoticed when spoken.

In contrast, grammatical errors can be necessary in dialogue, when such speech can be in character and therefore natural. In narrative they must be guarded against.

Equal diligence must be applied to punctuation. The omission of commas or parentheses, or any other necessary mark, can convey a totally different meaning from the one intended. The following paragraph from a Reuter report, at the time of the publication of *Hemingway in Cuba*, is an object lesson:

> Photos show a young Fidel Castro and an already old Ernest Hemingway he was born in 1898 with wide relaxed smiles.

The insertion of omitted parentheses before and after the reference to his birth date will reveal what the paragraph was meant to say. Parentheses can be indicated by brackets, dashes, or commas; in this instance they were overlooked by the writer, the printer, or the proof-checker. Brackets would have served best although, even then, the construction would have been bad.

If spelling worries you (and even if it doesn't), arm yourself with a good dictionary. The O E D is generally quoted as the authority. If you are uncertain about any aspect of grammar and punctuation, take a day or evening refresher course at your local adult education centre and keep a good book on English grammar and syntax on your reference shelf. Even if you think you don't need it, dip into it now and then and you will discover not only that it makes fascinating reading, but how much you have forgotten and need to learn again.

Choosing a publisher

Never choose one at random. Check that you are sending your manuscript to one who is likely to consider the genre of fiction you have written. It is useless to send a lowbrow romantic novel to a company noted for its intellectual list. It is equally useless to send it, or any other type of novel, to one who publishes only non-fiction. It will merely reveal that you haven't done your homework.

So how do you find out publishers' requirements? First, study library shelves for publishers who produce novels of the category you are aiming for. If, however, the one you choose publishes them only rarely, and few in number, the chances there are plainly limited.

Librarians, particularly senior ones, are usually well informed about publishers' lists and helpful with information, and of course book shops are well worthy of a study. Book-sellers are often helpful and the reading room of your local library may well stock the trade publication *The Bookseller*; if not, ask for it at the information desk and an obliging librarian will probably let you browse through it on the premises. This publication will keep you up to date with the latest develop-ments in the publishing world; who is publishing what, which books are currently popular and, if you are alert, coming trends. It can be mailed to you weekly. The subscription is high but, again, it can be an investment.

The same applies to the *Writers' & Artists' Yearbook*, which lists not only United Kingdom publishers and publications, but others worldwide, together with articles by experts on all fields of authorship. Because the book contains so much information it would take continuous visits to the library to absorb it all, so this is another recommended investment to keep close beside your desk.

Finally, there is no reason why you should not write to a pub-lishing house, asking if you can obtain their catalogue. Some still send out copies, despite high production costs.

Submitting your work

Having decided on the publisher whom you would like to pub-lish your novel, how do you approach him?

Sending the completed novel used to be the norm and this method is still used by many established authors writing regularly for established publishers, letting the book speak for itself rather than submitting a synopsis, or a couple of opening chapters and a synopsis of the remainder – a practice currently favoured because it means far less work and less wasted time. Many pub-lishers now stipulate this method.

My own preference is for the first and more diligent approach because that was the way I started and have always practised, not only for personal satisfaction but because a story can change substantially in the course of writing and predicted developments fail to work out. I like to see it through to the end.

But time and economy govern changing systems and the submission of minimal opening chapters with a synopsis is now increasingly recommended in the pages of writing magazines and under publishers' requirements listed in the *Writers' & Artists' Yearbook* and *The Writer's Handbook*. For the author, one advantage of this time-saving system is the equal saving on postage and packing when making the initial approach, together with the obligatory enclosure of the same amount for return in case of rejection, but remember that such costs are expenses an author has to be prepared to meet. Another advantage is that the author should get a quicker decision.

From the publisher's or editor's viewpoint this 'curtain-raiser' type of submission enables them to judge the quality of writing and to assess plotting skill, but what it does not prove, as a fully completed novel does, is whether the new author can sustain the impetus of a chapter or two written in the first flush of enthusiasm.

The third method of approach, and one which seems to be increasing in popularity, is the submission of a Proposal which outlines the author's ideas for a novel and his or her qualifiations for writing it. However, producing an effective Proposal demands skill. Authoritative articles on this and other specific subjects appear from time to time in the leading writing magazines. The beginner would be wise to watch out for them. Alternatively, a letter to the Features Editor, enquiring about back numbers containing such articles and whether they are available for purchase, might be fruitful.

Making the approach

Which method you choose must be your own. Don't seek advice from too many others because everyone's ideas depend on their own experiences and may well conflict and confuse.

Let us imagine you have decided on the publisher you wish to be published by, also on your method of approach. If you choose to send a letter of enquiry first, make it brief. The same applies to a covering letter accompanying a typescript. Say what the story is about, its theme, its genre, and approximate length. If the background is a specialised one and you know it well, say so.

If you can truthfully say that a certain authority has read your book and has advised you to send it on his or her recommendation, do so if it can be substantiated, but although this might arouse a spark of interest it will avail you nothing if that spark doesn't ignite a similar reaction in the publisher or his professional readers. Don't say that your highborn relatives all declare you to be on a par with Galsworthy or Trollope (why should their birth qualify them as good judges of literature?), or that your friend Mabel adores it, or that you are sure it is right for their list because it is similar to one they recently published (that could be a very good reason for rejection!).

And don't be dogmatic: 'This novel is intelligent and well constructed and will interest intelligent people.' Don't be humble: 'I am approaching you diffidently but hopefully. . .' Don't be flattering: 'I can think of no other publisher who produces books to compare with the excellence of yours.' Don't be patronising: 'I have decided to let you have the chance to publish my work.' And don't be chatty or witty or pally.

If you think authors don't write letters like that, you're wrong.

Waiting for a decision

How long should you wait? This varies from publisher to publisher, but can be two or three months. This is reasonable; longer is not. Alarming stories are heard about inordinate delays, all of which may be true since publishers do receive a constant flow of manuscripts for consideration, many of which are then sent to outside readers for assessment. In the meantime the poor author waits in a state of tension. Does the silence mean that acceptance is being considered, or that the manuscript is lost? Hope vies with despair, and if no acknowledgement comes to hand (something not unknown, but not excusable), fear takes over.

Because of the uncertainty of the mail and the possibility of loss or non-delivery, some authors take the precaution of enclosing stamped self-addressed postcards along the following (imaginary) lines. This is particularly relevant to the magazine market:

> Sender's name and address
>
> 'Phone number
>
> Date
>
> It would be appreciated if you would sign and return this card to confirm the receipt of my manuscript entitled *The Desperate Dodo*, by I. B. Hopeful, despatched to you on .... (date).
>
> Date of receipt:......................................
>
> Signature on behalf of publishers:.......................................

Someone in the editorial office has only to fill in the blanks and send down to the mailing room, thus saving the publisher the trouble of dictating a letter of acknowledgment, and the author anxiety. I am told that the percentage of such acknowledgments is high.

If a decision is unduly prolonged, you are justified in enquiring about the current position, but do so politely, either by letter or 'phone. A letter addressed to the Fiction Editor is safer than a chat with an underling who promises to 'look into the matter and call you back', and never does.

Writing a synopsis

If you prefer to send a complete synopsis without any accompanying material, a few hints on its construction may be useful.

Writing one about a completed novel is no problem. It is all there before you, waiting to be condensed. Start with *brief* notes on each chapter, covering only the essential points, then proceed to an outline of the whole, keeping it as compact as possible.

Writing a synopsis of a book which has not yet been written is a different proposition. It can be unnerving for a reason already touched on – that many of us have only a vague idea of how the story will develop until we are actually writing it, when it swoops us up and carries us away, but since you have decided to proceed in a way that everyone tells you is 'the *right* one', here are the basic rules.

A synopsis is always written in the present tense. (*'Unlocking the door of his office, private eye Dick Jones is confronted with chaos. It has been burgled. He reaches for the 'phone and dials 999.'*)

Ensuing information must be equally concise because the synopsis must be kept to a minimum. This depends not only on the book's length but on the plot's complexities. A simple romance of 50,000 words could produce a synopsis of as little as 700–800, whereas an involved novel of 80–100,000 words could require from 1,000 to 1,500. The more compact but informative you can make your synopsis, the better. Stick to the bare bones and present your skeleton unadorned.

Protecting your titles

Contrary to the assumption that an author's title cannot be stolen, cases abound which prove otherwise.

I experienced it myself some years ago, when a friend who was branching out from journalism into fiction liked the title of one of my earlier novels, originally a magazine serial of which my book publishers had bought the volume rights. Not one that would have won the Booker prize, but a good seller in its field.

Some time later she had her first romantic novel published by a rival firm. It bore the same title. Mine was still on the library shelves. My attention was drawn to it by a City librarian who mentioned that the new *Shadows On The Sand* would not be ordered because duplicated titles confused borrowers and could be tiresome in library records. I learned that this decision was likely to be the same elsewhere.

So the person whose sales suffered was the author of the new book, who cheerfully admitted that she had liked the title so much that she had decided to use it and saw no reason why she should not. She was unconcerned about the libraries' viewpoint (there was no P. L. R. in those days) and thought the whole thing 'a bit of a giggle', until discovering that another adverse effect for her was the loss of follow-up paperback publication (even though her story resembled mine in no way at all) because a paperback edition of my book was still on the stands. So the person who cribbed the title was the loser.

Although she was largely to blame, her publishers were more so. Titles of books in print can always be checked, and as a precautionary measure it is publishing practice to do so. Titles can be changed at the outset before anything has been set up, in agreement between author and editor, but to do so later is a costly business. Had the new author and her publisher waited until my own book went out of print, they would have been on safer ground.

There is, as yet, no actual copyright on titles, but there are circumstances in which the use of a title can be restrained. The Society of Authors issues an excellent Quick Guide on the subject and I strongly advise all aspiring authors to get hold of it, along with the Society's other Quick Guides on important aspects of authorship and publishing. They are free to members, but sold to non-members at very modest prices. A list of these guides, which come in a handy booklet form, can be obtained direct from the Society. (Address listed at the end of this book.)

Because the subjects of **Copyright** and **Publishing Contracts** are too wide and too complex to be covered in detail in this book, I recommend Michael Legat's *A Writer's Rights,* which deals lucidly and comprehensively with both, as well as with many other aspects of publishing which baffle new writers.

Editorial changes

Because the copyright is yours, a publisher cannot alter your novel without your consent but, as already indicated, good copy editors can do a lot to improve books and I stick by my advice to heed suggestions – but note that heeding them does not mean accepting them blindly. You should consider them carefully, judging whether they really do improve your book. If you think they don't, then say so and point out why. Reasonable argument has often resulted in a good publishing relationship, each respecting the other's view.

If you are strongly averse to having a word altered, the choice is yours, but it is an unwise author who withdraws his book on a wave of indignation because his brain-child has been criticized.

If you can see no flaw and are somewhat resentful of your editor's comments, take a deep breath and think of the future. Presuming you are sure you have chosen the right publisher, and that you have already signed a contract and therefore cannot withdraw your book without creating dispute and ill-will, you will be wise to compromise. Not only alteratons in construction may be suggested, but changes in incidents to heighten drama or to sharpen a situation, but for the most part editorial requests will be for cutting, sometimes substantially, sometimes less so, and sometimes because the book is too long and therefore impossible to market at the price which has been carefully assessed for saleability. In the case of the latter, this assessment is usually made before acceptance and can be made conditional, so you will have had your chance to refuse at that point.

After acceptance, cutting is usually desirable for the reason already stressed – to improve your novel. This is where you settle down to amicable discussion with your editor, bearing in mind that just as a diamond cutter improves the quality of the stone, so can good cutting improve the quality of a novel. The need for cutting applies to most forms of writing and although the following story applies to journalism, it is nonetheless apt where over-writing is concerned in any field.

The story is traditionally quoted by American teachers of journalism and concerns a news editor who sent an inexperienced reporter to cover a flood in a place called Johnstown. Hours and hours of frustrated waiting passed, and no report came. The editor was becoming frantic when at last it began to come over the teletype, but on and on it went, printing out a melodramatic, 10,000-word story totally unsuited to newspaper reportage and opening with the line: 'God sits tonight in judgement at Johnstown.' Mercifully hanging on to a sense of humour, the editor wired back: 'Forget flood. Interview God.'

No copy editor will ask you to be as drastic as that with your cutting, but the story stresses the need to avoid killing your novel with over-writing.

Proof corrections

Not until proofs arrive will you see what your book is going to look like. You will receive two sets, one to be returned when checked and the other for your own use and on to which, if you are wise, you will meticulously copy every alteration. Since your novel is there in its entirety, paginated and presented just as it will appear when bound, and since the agreed alterations have been made, you cannot see why it should be necessary to check it all through again, but even so you are asked to do so and to return the proofs within a certain time.

It all looks splendid now it is in print, so you skim through it very happily – and shudder, when the final book arrives, to find some glaring printer's errors. Those errors must have been in the proofs, but 'somehow' passed unnoticed.

It is not the author's specific job to pick up literals, but you would be wise to keep an eye open for them. It is the easiest thing for them to escape tired editorial eyes (remember, your editor has been dealing with many other books besides yours and can become as weary as you). One howler which appeared in an American paperback edition of my novel, *Dragonmede*, leapt out of the first page. It had been correct in the original Simon & Schuster hardback, from which the paperback had been reproduced, so no further proof-reading had been involved nor should have been necessary; nevertheless the error leapt from the second paragraph.

The introductory one, quoted in an earlier chapter, indicated the mother's scandalous mode of living and because of this the second paragraph began, 'It wasn't surprising that visitors streamed to our tall terraced house in Bloomsbury. . .' . But the 'm' in 'streamed' had been changed to 'k' and this was at a time when streaking in public places was attracting much publicity. I blamed myself for not choosing another word, such as 'flocked'.

So read your proofs carefully. You will be limited in the amount of alterations you can do at this stage; anything over and above the limit stated in your contract will be charged to you because alterations after type has been set are costly. The insertion of one word into a sentence can mean re-setting a whole page and even a whole chapter, an operation no layperson can appreciate. And don't be upset if your single quotes have been altered to double, or *vice versa*, or the spelling of certain words has been changed, such as those ending in 'ise' (or 'ize'). Individual publishers have their own 'house style', sometimes reserving double quotes for quoted extracts and single for lines of dialogue (or yet again *vice versa*). The symbols used in proof correcting are clearly presented in the *Writers' & Artists' Yearbook* and in *The Oxford Dictionary for Writers and Editors*. You will find them fascinating to use.

13. Literary Agents

What does an agent do?

A really good one does a great deal.

Although I know well established authors to whom the very word 'agent' is anathema, they are usually the rare ones blessed with a faculty for business, which is probably why they see no reason for paying ten per cent commission for services they can render for themselves.

If you are one of the few creative people with a talent for financial wheeling and dealing, and with plenty of spare time in which to make contacts and handle business correspondence and all aspects of negotiation, then read no further. If you are not, the advantages of having an agent can be many. We'll take the good side first.

A really good agent knows the state of the market for he keeps in touch with leading publishers and should therefore be in a position to keep you in the picture regarding current trends and requirements. I say 'should' advisedly, because this is one of the main services for which authors employ agents while they themselves get on with the job of writing; but which has become a debatable point since the increase in genuine and so-called literary agents today.

A really good agent gives careful thought to a suitable publisher for your novel and equal thought to his promotion of your name when submitting it. He negotiates contracts, eliminates unfavourable clauses, ensures that the author's rights are preserved and knows his way around the minefield of copyright law. He chases dilatory publishers for decisions and negotiates the sale of many subsidiary rights both at home and abroad.

He is often successful in selling US rights, translation rights, and other media rights – frequently more lucratively than some publishers do (although this does not apply to many of the larger publishing houses who have Rights Departments and good world-wide representation).

A good agent also fulfils his responsibility to collect advances and royalties when due and to forward the balance promptly to the author. Only lax agents fall down in this respect. A freak story, but a true one, concerns a long established agency which failed to collect royalties from a publisher of reprint library editions until, five and a half years later, the author stumbled on the error and had to seek help from the Society of Authors.

It might be said that the author should have been more alert, but full-time authorship leaves little time for anything but writing, and in any case it is a contractual part of an agent's duties to handle the financial side exclusively.

So if you decide to employ an agent, check on such points at your first meeting and make sure they are confirmed in writing.

A good agent also strives to get improved terms with succeeding contracts, takes a genuine interest in his or her client and acts as a merciful buffer between author and publisher should there be any misunderstanding or dispute, thereby preventing the relationship from going sour and even preserving friendship between the two parties, both of whom know that their difference of opinion is solely a business one and not personal, but are aided by tactful mediation nonetheless.

On the other hand, a good agent also understands a publisher's problems. Some have even started their careers in publishing, which enables them to explain things which otherwise puzzle authors, to assess whether their complaints are justified, and to tactfully soothe anxiety.

That is the ideal picture and it does exist even though, today, the agency field is overcrowded and it is not easy to sort the wheat from the chaff. Swelling lists of agents advertise in writers' magazines, as well as in national newspapers, periodicals, and the Sunday press. Agents vie with agents for top-selling authors and mergers between agents, as with publishers, seem to be a sign of the times.

Agency fees

An agent normally charges ten per cent for services, plus VAT, but higher on foreign sales (usually twenty per cent). This is because sales are made through a co-operating agency resident in the respective overseas country. The foreign agent deducts his half of the commission and forwards the balance to the UK agent, sometimes after deduction of tax in the respective country and which is sometimes reclaimable or exempt if there is a tax agreement between the two respective countries. The UK agent then deducts his own commission, plus VAT, and forwards the rest to the author.

A good agent does not charge a reading fee for manuscripts submitted by prospective clients. Nor does a good agent charge any money until after the book is sold, when he takes his percentage on receipt of the publisher's advance on royalties, and thereafter on ensuing earnings. If he fails to find a publisher for your book, he gets nothing even though he has saved you the cost of postage on repeated submissions and possibly increased his telephone bill on your behalf. Remember that an agent has overheads, just as you do.

Literary agents, as in other forms of trading, exist to sell marketable goods. They have to assess possible profit within a reasonable period, and they will assess yours accordingly. If they turn you down, they may be making a mistake – or not. If they agree to represent you, give them a fair trial. Experienced agents know how to evaluate a manuscript in the light of current publishing trends, and even if your script is not wholly up to scratch they may take a chance on you.

The viewpoint of authors is more difficult because they can be sensitive to patronage or rebuff. Writers would not be writers if they were not sensitive, and a more understanding and sympathetic attitude from some agents who take a pride in being tough is particularly desirable.

On your part, don't expect too much. If an agent promises you the sky, don't pin your hopes on it. Romance writer Jean Saunders confirms this. 'Agents aren't miracle workers,' she warns, 'so don't be seduced by the talk of huge advances obtained by them. It may happen, but it's readability that will sell your book, whoever submits it.'

Adding that an agent can be a useful go-between, or a block to your own goals, she admits that she wound up her agent/author association when the agent objected to her writing non-fiction.

In contrast, many authors with big names give well-deserved credit to their agents. In my own experience, I have done the same whenever it has been well deserved.

Do book publishers give priority to agented authors?

A frequently expressed fear of many unpublished novelists is that no publishers will consider manuscripts from unagented authors. Proof that this is untrue comes from Carolyn Caughey, with whom I had a happy association when she edited the Fontana editions of my novels and is now Senior Editor at Hodder & Stoughton:

> 'We are delighted to look at submissions from agents or directly from authors themselves – some of our best-selling authors have no agents. But I would advise authors without agents to start by sending in about one hundred pages of typescript (double spaced on one side of the page, as ever) in the first instance, along with a short synopsis (one or two pages should be more than adequate).'

and from Broo Doherty, Senior Editor at Bantam Press:

> 'Most of our material comes in through agents, but we accept unsolicited manuscripts, all of which are considered. Unsolicited material should be typed, in double spacing, and photocopied. Please do not send the original copy. In the first instance it is recommended to submit the first few chapters of any book, with a detailed synopsis, rather than the whole work. It takes six to eight weeks for us to consider the material.'

With such encouragement, no author need be afraid to go it alone, but if you do decide to employ an agent and you do become dissatisfied with their services, or eventually feel you have been with them too long and have become taken-for-granted, you are free to go to another. You will naturally let the first agent know you are changing and he will be entitled to continuing commission on books he has sold for you, if the contracts he drew up have not expired. A parting can, and should, be amicable on both sides.

Summing up, an agent can be a godsend or a source of frustration. Much depends on the personalities and expectations of both.

How to find an agent?

One way is to study the list featured in the *Writers' & Artists' Yearbook* or *The Writer's Handbook*. Look for those bearing an asterisk, indicating that they are members of The Association of Authors' Agents, a professional body to whose standards members are expected to conform. However, this can be misleading since agents are not compelled to join the organization and several long established and reputable ones, some of whom existed before the Association was formed, have never done so, so the asterisk does not actually guarantee that only the best and most experienced are amongst its members.

Some publishers' catalogues indicate the names of literary agents with whom they negotiated individual titles. Count those handled by each named agent and then decide whether to approach the one responsible for the sale of the largest number, or one who has agented books of your chosen genre. Also bear in mind that an agent listed for only one or two may be an individual operator with a smaller list of clients to whom he can give more personal attention. The catalogue at least testifies to his ability to sell to a leading publisher so you won't be 'choosing blind', as some aspiring authors unhappily do from classified advertisements designed to entice them into enrolling with unheard-of agents operating from somewhere like Little Middleton On The Mud.

From choice, go for London agents because they are situated close to the leading publishers, circulate amongst them, and should have their ears to the ground.

If you have never been published, and do decide to approach an agent, you will need to submit a synopsis and a specimen chapter as an example of your writing ability. If you have already been published, enclose brief but pertinent details and a sample of published work.

However experienced or inexperienced you are, don't overload your covering letter with irrelevant information about yourself. You can indicate the theme and background of your novel, but remember that at this stage the agent is interested only in your work and your potential.

Should you be turned down by the bigger agencies, you will obviously have to focus your sights on lesser known ones. Here again, be careful. A deplorable situation exists in this country, as well as in others, wherein people with or without agency experience and with little knowledge of the literary world, can set themselves up as agents, advertising as such and as 'advisers' and 'literary consultants'. So take it slowly, listen carefully, and you will develop an instinct for the real and the phoney.

Agents and the women's magazines

I had never heard of literary agents until my first day in an editorial office, when I saw a junior sub-editor dividing a stock of manuscripts into two piles. One was the slush pile, the other from agents.

Contrary to a belief which is still held today, items from the slush pile were rarely put aside without a glance, though in many cases one reading of the first page was enough to indicate its quality or suitability. The really dog-eared ones told their own sad tale, as did those with freshly ironed title pages, or sometimes newly typed ones followed by others that needed to be. This taught me the folly of handicapping a story through bad or indifferent presentation.

Very logically, submissions from agents who could be relied on to send something worth considering would have prior consideration, as would those from agents representing established authors.

I soon learned that the time factor also played a part. With four magazines to cater for, the Literary Editor for the group wasted no time in hunting down suitable fiction, so reliable agents were a godsend.

This did not mean that outside submissions were never accepted, for even in slush piles undiscovered gems can lie. So exacting was this search for the right fiction that every member of the staff (including myself, then secretary to the Managing Editor of the group) had to read submissions in addition to routine editorial work, and a time limit was set on their written reports. First reader, one week, to include a brief synopsis of the story and a comment, for or against. Second reader, more experienced, one week and lengthier comments with a personal opinion. Third reader (nearer in rank to the Literary Editor) again one week, with a critical summing up and a personal verdict.

All three judgements were independent of each other and, with the manuscript, had to be on the Literary Editor's desk within a month for her consideration and final reading – unless previous readings had been unanimously for or against, and particularly if they were strongly divided, when the final judgement would be her own.

Taking a stack of manuscripts home for weekend reading by all staff was taken for granted. In this way a promising writer, whether agented or not, was rarely allowed to slip through the net, but fishing in well stocked agency waters invariably yielded a better catch.

Today the editorial scene is vastly different. Drastic economy cuts have reduced some staffs to a minimum of overworked people. The official rank of Literary Editor seems to have disappeared and in many magazine offices even an official Fiction Editor appears to have gone the same way, though letters or submissions need to be addressed to them to focus on the right department. This does not mean that attention given to fiction is less, but that the responsibility is shared by the reduced and overworked staff.

In some cases, fiction is handled by a part-timer coming to the office two or three days weekly and continuing to work at pressure at home for the rest of the week. Meanwhile, in all cases, the space available for fiction is becoming smaller and smaller.

Despite this, the deluge of manuscripts, numbering up to several hundred a month in some magazine offices, is often too heavy a load to be dealt with by minimal staff, so some magazines employ a nucleus of agents to find the stories they want. This means that some magazines no longer consider unsolicited manuscripts.

Unfortunately many agents only handle short stories if they are already handling the author's novels, so more and more writers have to freelance. There is an eternal cry of, 'If *only* I could find an agent!' from many beginners who have been knocking on agents' doors unsuccessfully. Yet the situation is not without hope. More and more people are writing successfully and profitably today. The secret is to find out exactly which markets do consider unsolicited work, and to study them constantly and carefully.

Magazine guidelines

Most publications produce editorial guidelines, but a few, like those relying on agents, have ceased to. Therefore, when you read 'no unagented submissions' or 'no unsolicited manuscripts considered' beneath listed publications in the valuable section on UK newspapers and magazines in the *Writers' & Artists' Yearbook*, save yourself time and postage by concentrating on those who still do.

These include leading short story markets like *Woman's Weekly, My Weekly, Peoples' Friend, Best, Bella, Take a Break* and others. You can obtain these guidelines by application, but make your request brief and polite and don't forget the obligatory stamped and self-addressed envelope – not too small, for those from the long-standing and big-selling *Woman's Weekly* run to two and a half pages and even include the sympathetic line: '*We cannot offer criticism, but if your short story or serial shows promise, we will contact you and suggest alterations.*'

To this I can add personal words of encouragement from Gaynor Davies of *Woman's Weekly*: 'Our policy is always to encourage writers, and despite receiving approximately 600–900 unsolicited manuscripts per month all are considered and unsuitable ones are rejected with fair and helpful comment.'

She also stresses the importance of reading the magazine on a regular basis over several weeks before submitting anything, adding, 'This is the only sure way to get the feel of our fiction.' No words could be wiser, and should be heeded by male writers as well as female for the feminine viewpoint is radically different today, opening up opportunities for male authors in magazines hitherto regarded as exclusively feminine territory. Many masculine names appear regularly in such publications.

As for serials, though their heyday has declined, markets for them do still exist. *Woman's Weekly, My Weekly,* and *Peoples' Friend,* to name but three, offer opportunities (the last two come from the publishers, D C Thomson of Dundee.) The two-parter has replaced the serial in many magazines, such as the long-standing and respected *Woman's Realm.*

Woman's Own, on the other hand, once a prolific publisher of short stories and serials, sadly report that they can no longer accept unsolicited fiction for the reasons mentioned earlier, but they still encourage fiction writers with an annual short story competition which can lead to publication.

Despite staff reorganizations and policy changes, and unsolicited submissions being far too many to cope with in what appears to be the majority of cases, there still remains cause for optimism. New writers who cast their nets wide *are* getting into print, and payments are high, but that means no relaxation of the ever-vital market study – not only of published fiction, but of features and advertisements and readers' letters, all of which indicate the lifestyles of varying magazine readers.

Features on trendy fashions and make-up, true-life stories about marriage and parental problems, age-related health problems, rebellious letters from teenagers, worried letters from young wives and mothers, proud letters from doting grandmothers – all clearly project the readership of individual magazines and the various social levels fiction writers can cater for.

Advertisements, in particular, reveal readership age and income groups. Those for stair-lifts or reclining chairs or motorized scooters speak for themselves; features on cosmetic surgery accompanied by advertisements for fashionable clinics are plainly aimed at a middle-aged and moneyed readership, while down-to-earth articles on home economy, family interests and motherhood, sometimes supported by 'special offers' of advertised goods, obviously cater for the young marrieds.

Travel features as well as travel advertisements are splendid signposts, ranging from economical and not too strenuous coach trips for older people, to more expensive skiing trips abroad for the young, and even more luxurious holidays for the middle-aged and well heeled.

Never let up on market study if you hope to see an end to rejections.

The changing world of women's magazines

For 'then-and-now' comparisons one has only to examine a copy of the high ranking monthly, *Woman's Journal*. Founded in 1927, with a portrait on the cover of Her Majesty the Queen Mother when she was the young Duchess of York, it remained amongst her favourite reading even after she became Queen. On one memorable occasion she even wrote, through her lady-in-waiting, to express surprise that a certain advertisement should be included in the pages of a respected magazine which she had always read and enjoyed. The offending advertisement was dropped and a tactful letter of apology and appreciation was written but, although concerned, the editor was delighted by this evidence that Her Majesty read the *Journal* so thoroughly.

Fiction was a big feature of the glossy *Journal* in those days.

With several good short stories per issue and serialisation of outstanding novels by outstanding authors like H E Bates and Agatha Christie and Dornford Yates and Georgette Heyer, it was a wonderful read at a shilling a month (first launched at six old pence). Now, though admirably produced, it has become another glossy magazine in a line-up of glossies, with no room for fiction.

Change is always inevitable, but never has there been change so drastic as that wrought by the German magazines, *Bella, Best, Take a Break* and *Hello,* brought to the UK in the late eighties by their publishers, H Bauer and Gruner & Jahr. Prior to that, women's magazines published short stories of up to 5,000 and even 6,000 words, often romantic but now scorned as 'sentimental' – though they were frequently true to life and written by renowned authors of the day, male and female.

The 'German invasion' of the UK publishing world changed all that. Stories of around 5,000 words rapidly yielded place to 1,500 words, then 1,000 and now even as low as 500. The popularity of the quicky tale or the coffee-break story had arrived. So had the 'entertainment' magazine, of which *Take a Break* is a case in point. In a recent 59-page issue only two single-page stories appeared, with most of the page taken up by illustration. Even two short stories was one more than in some rival magazines.

But there is a good side to all this – the direct contact which short story writers now have with editors can be valuable and stimulating, whereas the distance-barrier between editors and freelance writers was once a difficult bridge to cross. The curt rejection slip now seems a thing of the past, so hopeful authors need not be afraid of making an approach provided that they are courteous, keep it short, and appreciate that an editor's time is as valuable as their own.

An additional advantage of self-representation is that with the growth of the European Common Market, opportunities for sales to countries within it, both of short stories and articles, have increased and can be done either through syndication or personal approach. The latter is simplified for British writers because English is the main EU business language. For full information on this exciting development for writers, read Barbara Wood-Kaczmar's valuable feature in the *Writers' & Artists' Yearbook.*

Authors and the Internet

For writers with access to the Internet, surfing through the many sites on the World Wide Web in search of new markets for print publication can be rewarding. Because it demands time and patience, this is a service no agent is likely to do for you, but 'it is an excellent way to sample magazines and journals that you have difficulty in getting hold of', says expert Phillip J Conran in *Writers' Monthly*. 'Many now have web pages that contain enough information to give you a good feel for what they publish, and most give submission guidelines. If you have an e-mail address, you can contact them directly and have the added benefit of being in touch with your prospective editor almost immediately.'

14. Other Publishing Channels

Self-publishing

Since desk top publishing enabled writers to produce slim volumes of poetry for circulation amongst friends and family, or specialised booklets to sell by mail order, or short histories of charities to boost fund-raising and the like, digital printing has revolutionised self-publishing to such a degree that trying to compete in the market place need now be no deterrent *provided that the author realises the full extent of his personal commitment.*

Richard Bell, editor of *Writers News* and *Writing Magazine,* sums it up well when saying, '. . .let us be clear what we mean by self-publishing. It is where an author takes on to their own shoulders the responsibility for producing and marketing their own book. . . this is a lot of work, but it can also be exciting, enjoyable and satisfying.'

Encouragement also comes from famous names in literary history who launched their careers by self-publishing – Horace Walpole, Balzac, John Galsworthy, Rudyard Kipling, Beatrix Potter, Lewis Carroll, J M Barrie, Mark Twain, D H Lawrence, Upton Sinclair, Zane Grey, Alexander Pope, Robbie Burns, Virginia Woolf (who founded the Hogarth Press) and William Blake, who even made his own ink and hand printed the pages while poor Mrs Blake laboriously stitched on the covers.

To these are now added names like Timothy Mo, with his self-published novel *Brownout on Breadfruit Boulevard* and Jill Paton Walsh's *Knowledge of Angels,* short-listed for the Booker Prize, and Rupert Allason, MP, author of espionage and political intrigue novels as Nigel West and who set up St Ermin's Press 'in protest against the failure of established publishers to market that type of fiction properly'.

All this sounds rather easy until you get down to the nitty gritty behind Richard Bell's sound analysis of an author's personal commitment. This includes 'producing and marketing your book: editing, book design, cover design, typesetting, print and production, selling – and all the details right down to invoicing and accounting'.

If you do propose to handle all management aspects yourself, these other details should be well heeded for they include advertising, publicity, storage, delivery, distribution, out-on-the-road expenses when being your own commercial traveller, and their time equation in loss or neglect of other work.

Financial outlay will particularly concern those short of cash, so it is important to investigate that side first. Jill Paton Walsh is quoted as saying that unless you can afford to lose more than £4,000 and spend all your time on marketing the book, publishing it yourself can be a dangerous venture. This may well be true if you overspend at the outset by ordering a few thousand copies just because, the larger the order, the smaller the unit price, but digital printing now enables a self-publisher to test the market with as few as two or three hundred. This is an asset for, as orders grow, extra copies can be run off quickly and economically. Another asset is the existence of commercial companies to relieve self-publishers of many of the more onerous tasks.

So how do you get started?

The first thing to consider is the type of book you propose to publish. That non-fiction is the safest bet is widely confirmed by booksellers and distributors despite the two successful novels mentioned earlier, both of which were by well launched and well established names and, in one case, by an author previously experienced in self-publishing.

The truth is that a novel needs a strong sales pitch and well organized distribution behind it. Good promotion and distribution are costly and, today, fiction needs these services more than any other literary category. Falling fiction sales to libraries confirm this, as does the increased shelf space given to non-fiction, both in shops and libraries. So start by playing safe, unless you have no financial worries.

How to go about it

First – **Research.** Read all you can lay your hands on about self-publishing. Series articles in writing magazines can form a tuition course in themselves and books on the subject are recommended later in this chapter. Learn about the different parts of a book so that you know what printers are talking about when they refer to *dummy*, *prelims*, *verso*, *recto*, *point size*, *literal*, *typo*, *PMTs*, *tranny*, *running head*, and many more terms incomprehensible to the layman. Get hold of Ann Kritzinger's 'print-speak' list; study it and learn.

Visits to booksellers will form an important part of your research. Buy samples of current books in a style in which you would like your book to appear. Ask for the manager or the buyer and talk to him. If you are hesitant or shy, strive to overcome it because booksellers can be good sources of information and advice.

Next, take your complete typescript and sample books to several printers and get quotations. Printers are listed in the Yellow Pages, and some advertise in various writers' magazines. Many may be worth contacting, but go carefully. I once attended a much publicised meeting for would-be self-publishers and was astonished when a leading speaker, described in the programme as a professional printer 'of high standing', revealed ignorance of a vital copyright law in relation to his craft. Examining a beautifully produced non-fictional book, of which the author had reclaimed all rights when the original publishers became part of a merger, the man declared airily that he could easily produce another edition simply by photographing it, including the illustrations.

He was astonished to learn that copyright in the typography remained with the original publisher and that both he and the author would be in legal trouble if infringing it. So tread carefully and check on all so-called 'experts' before heeding them.

Once you have decided on your cover design and your printer, test the market by taking advance prints of your book's cover to all booksellers in your area and beyond. Again digital printing has made the cost of such prints economical.

Counting the cost

Never leave it entirely to a printer to produce your book. *You* must control its appearance. Those which sell are those which stand out visually, so don't stint on the cover, in terms of both time and money. Look at the eye-catching ones in booksellers' windows and on table displays within shops. This way you'll keep on learning.

How to sell? With hard work and persistence. That means no days off, except Sundays spent on accountancy. It also means devoting time to the job instead of writing your next book. Non-writing time is time wasted, so the sensible alternative is to employ a professional salesman with flair. Add to your outlay another 12% or slightly more for his commission, in addition to the normal booksellers' 35% discount. You can advertise for a freelance representative in *The Bookseller*, or look in the trade section of Cassell's *Directory of Publishing*. All this may seem daunting, but experienced self-publishers report that it is money well spent.

You will be liable for all packing and delivery charges. Post free applies only to single orders, on which, I am told, you can stipulate a lower discount of around 25%. Reject any 'sale or return' requests, which mean that buyers pay only for what they sell and then only after they've sold it. And bear in mind that returned copies may well be shop-soiled, resaleable only at a reduced or remainder price. And note that you may need to add another 33% to your total costs to cover distribution, promotion, and complimentary copies to essential sources. You should also send out plenty of review copies, accompanied by a leaflet stating selling price and publisher's name and address.

You must also send depositing copies, as dictated by the Copyright Acts, to all of the following: The British Library; The Bodleian Library, Oxford; The University Library, Cambridge; The National Library of Scotland; The Library of Trinity College, Dublin and The National Library of Wales. These mandatory copies must be sent within one month of publication.

One copy must also be sent to the Legal Deposit Office at the British Library, Boston Spa, Wetherby, West Yorkshire LS23 7BY. Data on your book will then be used in bibliographic services and the book itself will eventually be made available to the public as part of a national printed archive.

Another essential is an International Standard Book Number (ISBN), a bibliographic code for all individual books and a quick form of identification for booksellers and librarians. They are issued free by the Standard Book Numbering Agency, 12 Dyott Street, London WC1A 1DF.

The foregoing is only part of a self-publishing operation. For more, read Ann Krizinger's *Bring it to Book* (Scriptmate edition, 1997), Charles Foster's *Editing, Design and Book Production*

(Journeyman, 1993) and, for information on copyright and other vital aspects of publishing, Michael Legat's *The Writer's Rights* (A & C Black, 1995).

Vanity publishing

In no way must self-publishing be confused with vanity publishing. The latter is an invidious practice universally condemned.

Vanity publishers' advertisements usually run along these lines:

> **Authors** – are you looking for a publisher? If your book deserves publication, expanding publishers would like to hear from you. Write to: . . .

That is slightly more subtle than many, and therefore more beguiling. It suggests that they, as publishers, are seeking books which are worth publishing and will consider your manuscript and honestly assess it. In reality, they will praise it and accept it however bad it is.

Here I quote the *Writers' and Artists' Yearbook*:

> In their effort to secure business, vanity publishers will usually give exaggerated praise to an author's work and arouse equally unrealistic hopes of its commercial success. However, when authors pay vanity publishers they are paying simply for the manufacture of copies. True publishers invest *their own money* in the whole publishing process. . . editorial, design, manufacturing, selling, distribution. The vanity publisher invests *the author's* money in but one part of the process: manufacture.
>
> The distressing reports we have received from embittered victims of vanity publishers underline the importance of reading extremely carefully the contracts offered by such publishers. Often these will provide for the printing of, say, 2000 copies of the book, usually at a quite exorbitant cost to the author, but will leave the 'publisher' under no obligation to bind more than a very limited number. Frequently, too, the author will be expected to pay the cost of any effective advertising, while the 'publisher' makes little or no effort to promote the distribution and sale of the book. Again, the names and imprints of vanity publishers are well known to literary editors, and their productions therefore are rarely, if

ever, reviewed or even noticed in any important periodical. Similarly, such books are hardly ever stocked by booksellers.

The result of such dealings is that the author is landed with a mass of printed pages and only a few copies of a cheaply jacketed book which, to a bookseller, speaks for itself. The author has therefore to hand over more money to have the loose pages stitched and bound to match those of the vanity publisher, only to find that no one will look at a shoddy product.

15. Organizations and Societies for Authors

It is not surprising that writers sometimes wish to escape from the isolation of their work and to seek the company of others similarly employed.

Many clubs and societies fulfil this purpose. A large section covering **Societies, Prizes and Festivals** is featured in the *Writers' & Artists' Yearbook*, amongst which the following are but a few:

The Society of Authors: founded in 1884 with the object of representing, assisting, and protecting authors. Its scope includes specialist associations for translators, broadcasters, educational, medical, technical and children's writers. Members are entitled to legal aid as well as general advice in connection with the marketing of their work, contracts, choice of publisher, etc. Publishes *The Author* quarterly. It also issues a series of booklets on aspects and problems of authorship, issued free to members and at a nominal price to non-members. Address: 84 Drayton Gardens, London, SW10 9SB.

International P.E.N. is a world association of writers, founded in 1921 under the presidency of John Galsworthy and designed to uphold the rights of authors and to promote international good will through the medium of literature. The initials originally stood for Poets, Playwrights, Editors, Essayists and Novelists, but membership is now open to all published writers, including translators, irrespective of sex, creed or race, providing they subscribe to its fundamental principles. Congresses are held in varying countries and individual centres hold regular meetings and literary events. Address of the English centre: 7 Dilke Street, London SW3 4JE.

The Writers' Guild of Great Britain is affiliated to the TUC and represents writers' interests in film, radio, television, theatre and publishing. Originally the Screenwriters' Guild, the union now includes all areas of freelance writing. Address: 430 Edgware Road, London W2 1EH.

Authors' Licensing and Collecting Society Ltd (ALCS), Isis House, 74 New Oxford Street, London WC1A 1EF. Set up in 1977 to collect and distribute money to writers for payments which authors and other copyright holders are unable to collect individually. Membership of this valuable organization is vital to authors and successor membership extends to their heirs. The Society of Authors and the Writers' Guild of Great Britain are represented on its Council of Management.

Public Lending Right (PLR). Under the PLR system, payment is made from public funds to authors (writers, translators, illustrators and some editors/compilers) whose books are lent out from public libraries. Payment is made once a year, in February, and the amount authors receive is proportional to the number of times (established from a sample) that their books were borrowed during the previous year (July to June). The author must register titles of published books, with their ISBN numbers, with the Registrar of Public Lending Right, Bayheath House, Prince Regent Street, Stockton-on-Tees, Cleveland TS18 1DF.

The Society of Women Writers and Journalists, founded in 1894 for women writers of all genre. President: Nina Bawden, CBE FRSL. Lectures, monthly lunch-time meetings and workshops, free literary advice for members, annual Weekend School. Publishes *The Woman Journalist* quarterly. Hon. Secretary, Jean Hawkes, 110 Whitehall Road, Chingford, London E4 6DW.

Women Writers Network (1985). London-based network serving both salaried and independent women writers from all disciplines, and providing a forum for the exchange of information, support and networking opportunities. Holds monthly meetings and workshops. Publishes a newsletter and members' directory. Information from Susan Kerr, 55 Burlington Lane, London W4 3ET.

The Crime Writers' Association. For professional writers of crime novels, short stories, plays, and serious works on crime. Associate membership is open to publishers, journalists, and booksellers specialising in crime literature. Publishes *Red Herrings* monthly (for members only). Address: PO Box 10772, London N6 4SD.

Book Trust exists to open up the world of books and reading to people of all ages and cultures. Its services include the Book Information Service, a unique, specialist information and research service for all queries on books and reading. Book

Trust administers a number of literary prizes, including the Booker Prize, and produces a wide range of books, pamphlets and leaflets. Address: Book House, 45 East Hill, Wandsworth, London SW18 2QZ.

The Authors Club (at the Arts Club) 40 Dover Street, London W1X 3RB. Founded 1891 by Sir Walter Besant; welcomes as members writers, publishers, critics, journalists, academics and anyone involved with literature.

Regional Arts Associations exist to promote and develop the arts, including literature, in their regions. For addresses see the *Writers' & Artists Yearbook.*

Writers' Circles – an easy way to get to know fellow writers in your area, both published and unpublished. The standards of ability and enthusiasm will vary from group to group, but it may be worth your while to find out if there is one within reach. A nationwide Directory of Writers' Circles is obtainable from: Jill Dick, Oldacre, Horderns Park Road, Chapel-en-le-Frith, High Peak SK23 9SY.

Residential courses

Many residential writers' courses are held up and down the country. They are usually moderately priced (according to accommodation and facilities) and offer tuition, workshops, discussion groups and lectures. Prominent amongst these are the five day courses run by The Arvon Foundation, available to people over the age of 16. They are held at three centres based in Devon, Yorkshire and Invernesshire. Tuition is by working writers. For the three addresses see the *Writers' & Artists' Yearbook.*

Courses for weekends or longer have become increasingly popular in recent years and have even spread overseas to France and the Greek islands. Many authors make them their annual holidays. In the UK they include the long-established Writers' Summer School held at the Swanwick Conference Centre, Swanwick, Derbyshire, the Annual Writers' Conference at King Alfreds' University College, Winchester, and the *Sunday Times* literary gathering at Hay-on-Wye.

Increasingly, and deservedly, popular is the Southern Writers Conference at Earnley, Chichester, West Sussex; close to the sea and set in beautiful grounds, it's facilities, accommodation and cuisine are hard to beat. The programme is lively and includes top speakers. (Secretary: Lucia White, Stable House, Home Farm, Coldharbour Lane, Dorking, Surrey RHA 3JG.)

A fuller range of courses up and down the country are regularly announced, and advertised, in writers' magazines.

Books for authors

Earlier, I advised aspiring authors to build their own 'working library'. Here are a few basic titles from my own bookshelves which will make a good start:

The Shorter Oxford English Dictionary – the standard twelve volume edition condensed into two.

The Oxford Dictionary for Writers and Editors.

Roget's Thesaurus (Penguin).

An Author's Guide to Publishing, Michael Legat, Robert Hale.

A Writer's Rights, Michael Legat, A & C Black.

The Writer's Handbook, Macmillan.

The Oxford Dictionary of Quotations.

The Oxford Dictionary of English Proverbs.

Brewer's Dictionary of Phrase and Fable, Cassell. This can be an excellent source for ideas as well as for checking facts – and it makes beguiling reading.

Research for Writers, Ann Hoffmann, A & C Black.

Usage and Abusage, Eric Partridge, Hamish Hamilton.

The Penguin Dictionary of Historical Slang, Eric Partridge.

Modern English Usage, Fowler, Oxford University Press.

Cassell's Classified Quotations, Gurney Benham. Being classified under subjects, this is recommended for quick and convenient access.

Encyclopaedia of Superstitions, Christina Hole, Ed: Radford Hutchinson.

Larousse Encyclopaedia of Modern History, from 1500 to the present day. Useful for quick reference, but not in-depth.

And topping the list, the ultimate encyclopaedia for authors, *Microsoft ENCARTA, World English Edition*, conveniently produced on CD Rom and with the added advantage of new material yearly.

The above titles will form the nucleus of a *basic* reference library, but you are sure to add to them (the process never ceases). In the meantime they will supplement wider research in specialised libraries – such as the London Library, 14 St James's Square, London SW1Y 4LG, where members may take out ten books at a time (fifteen for country members). Books may be ordered by post, but postage must be met in both directions.

Subscribers have access to the stacks, the use of a comfortable reading room, and may purchase the printed author catalogue and subject index volumes for home reference – a boon if you live at a distance and wish to order by post or by 'phone.

The staff are extremely helpful. On several occasions they have carefully selected for me a range of titles on specific subjects in response to a 'phone call, and sent them first class to ensure delivery the next day. The current subscription of £80 may seem high, but for such a service it is not – and remember, it can be set against a professional author's tax. Short-term subscriptions are available on application. These can be useful if you are on a brief visit to London and want to do some on-the-spot research.

Major provincial cities, also leading cities in Scotland, Wales and Ireland, have libraries on a par with the main London ones, so wherever you live you can be within reach of excellent research sources. The difference between the historic London Library and others is that its collection of rare books is unmatched.

Periodicals for authors (mail order)

The Author (quarterly), published by The Society of Authors, 84 Drayton Gardens, London SW10 9SD
Writers News (monthly), PO Box 4, Nairn IV12 4HU *Writing Magazine* (bi-monthly), PO Box 4, Nairn IV12 1HU

UK magazines (short story markets)

Woman's Weekly, IPC Magazines, King's Reach Tower, Stamford Street, London SE1 9LS

Woman's Realm, IPC Magazines, King's Reach Tower, Stamford Street, London SE1 9LS

Woman, IPC Magazines, King's Reach Tower, Stamford Street, London SE1 9LS

Woman & Home, IPC Magazines, King's Reach Tower, Stamford Street, London SE1 9LS

My Weekly, D C Thomson & Co. Ltd., 80 Kingsway East, Dundee DD4 8SL

People's Friend, D C Thomson & Co. Ltd., 80 Kingsway East, Dundee DD4 8SL

Bella, G & J of the UK, 25–27 Camden Road, London NW1 9LL

Best, G & J of the UK, Portland House, Stag Place, London SW1E 5AB

Take A Break, H. Bauer Publishing, 25–27 Camden Road, London NW1 9LL

Chat, IPC Magazines, King's Reach Tower, Stamford Street, London SE1 9LS

That's Life!, H. Bauer Publishing, 25–27 Camden Road, London NW1 9LL

Yours, Choice Publications, Apex House, Oundle Road, Peterborough PE2 9NP

– and finally, that long established weekly which holds it own, and its individuality, despite all competition, *The Lady,* still at the address it has occupied since I walked by its doors as a teenager: 39–40 Bedford Street, London WC2E 9ER.

Index